Rowing from the inside out

Rowing from the inside out

Jonathan Drake

The Art of Indoor Rowing
with on-the-water in mind

'Rowing is one of the best fitness activities you can do, but *Rowing from the inside out* will stretch your mind as well, helping you achieve better self-awareness and 'feel' – essential ingredients if you want to become good on a rowing machine or try the sport on the water.'

Robin Williams, MBE, former Olympic coach

'A well-structured approach to optimum training for beginners and experienced rowers with an emphasis on developing and refining the skill and craft of rowing while making the most of using a rowing machine. Drake draws heavily upon his expertise and knowledge of The Alexander Technique and Tai Chi to help avoid injury and maximize the potential for success.'

Theresa Batty, former lightweight national team sculler, competitive long-distance open water sculler, senior (and former head) coach at Lake Washington Rowing Club, yoga instructor, ski instructor

Jonathan Drake's *'Rowing from the inside out* is a book that any rower can benefit from including in their library. It's a valuable resource for rowers and coaches alike, whether recreational or competitive. Drake's book incorporates practical exercises for truly rowing 'with your body,' along with simple yet skilful explanations that will deliver insights at all levels of the sport. In my experience it's unique. I haven't come across such a self-help book, which is not only about rowing, but also about movement in general. Highly recommended!'

Oli Rosenbladt, Junior Head Rowing Coach at Duxbury Maritime School and journalist at row2k.com

'Jonathan Drake´s perspective on mastering the rowing stroke emphasizes mindful exploration over mindless repetition. As he recognizes that movements are always generated "from the inside out," Drake guides his readers through exercises designed to help them understand their own physicality and the impact of their mindset on movement quality.

Although addressed to novices starting with rowing (indoors and outdoors), his book is also particularly beneficial for athletes returning to rowing after a break or injury, or any situation that demands a more reflective approach instead of doing "more of the same." Coaches, who might be interested in what causes their athletes difficulties to "sit up tall" or "engage the hips," will also find value in its starting points and insights. This book is an invaluable resource.'

Stefanie Buller, Alexander teacher and movement coach working with elite rowers

'By applying two proven body practices – the Alexander Technique and Tai-chi – to an understanding of rowing technique, the rowing action is taken to a new level of quality in *Rowing from the inside out*. You can practise this old form of movement with ease and strength, mindfulness and speed and, above all, great fun. With the help of this book, rowing, both in the gym and on water, could become, like cycling, a healthy and environmentally-friendly sport and leisure activity for everyone.

Jonathan Drake is a body and movement expert who specialises in fundamental forms of human locomotion: running, swimming and rowing. His extensive knowledge and wide-ranging experience in this field is based on his deep enthusiasm for the natural design of the human body.'

Bernd Dahlhaus, Alexander Technique trainee, music teacher and systemic consultant

'I highly recommend this unique, in-depth, mind-body resource for anyone starting out rowing or who wants to improve their technique.'

Gavin Langford, Art of Swimming teacher and rowing coach

'I have known Jonathan for 25 years as an Alexander Technique teacher, Teacher of Tai-chi; always wanting to develop more; adding the Shaw method of swimming and the Balk method of running to his teaching. When Jonathan was introduced to rowing, his knowledge in Alexander Technique Teaching and Tai-chi awakened the possibility to further develop the teaching of Rowing.

He then thought, read, analyzed the concept and stripped it back to the basic building blocks. It was then rebuilt into bite-sized pieces for the lay person, to understand how to put the building blocks together for themselves. They start the process of using their bodies to sit, stand, move in an easy, energy efficient, balanced, new patterned, body aware way, to master rowing. It takes time, thought, knowledge, testing, and repeated practice to understand all the elements that make up one stroke in rowing, which involves the whole body, but Jonathan has done just that.

Rowing from the inside out does exactly what the title says. I hope this text will be read and used in the gym for inside rowers. However, it is for all rowers, experienced or those starting on their sporting journeys, to prevent incorrect movements, habits, and instead teach the fluidity of rowing that Jonathan has found in this amazingly 'simple', but detailed understanding of the body's anatomy and functional makeup, its energy, the breath, working with the natural movement, which is so delicately formed into a teaching, learning mode for everyone to follow.'

Yvonne Ayliffe, osteopath for 43 years, D.O, Paed.Ost.Dip., FSCCO, GOsC, Consultant RMTi

Dedicated to:

My father, **John Drake** (1916 – 1986), a club rower in his youth. As a family we would watch the Oxford and Cambridge Boat Race. He never tried to impose his early passion for rowing on his skinny little boy who was more interested in football and tennis at the time. I now roam the same waterway in a single shell that he rowed on in a four or eight.

Patrick Pearson (1954 – 2020), Alexander teacher and rowing coach, who inspired me to take up rowing late in life.

Frank Cunningham (1922 – 2013), coach at Lake Washington Rowing Club, Seattle, USA, who eloquently describes the art of sculling in his classic book *The Sculler at Ease*. His words continue to inspire my efforts to be a better sculler.

Rowing from the inside out

For information, contact: rowingfromtheinsideout@gmail.com

British Library Cataloguing-in-Publication data

A catalogue record for this book is available from the British Library.

ISBN 978-1-0686621-1-9

Design and layout by Kaarin Wall

Foreword

Rowing from the Inside Out by Jonathan Drake is an excellent guide that transcends the typical instructional fitness book, offering a comprehensive and holistic approach to mastering the art of indoor rowing. Jonathan Drake, an experienced indoor rowing coach and sculler, weaves his expertise in the Alexander Technique and Tai Chi into the fabric of this beautifully illustrated book, creating a unique resource for both beginners and seasoned rowers alike.

The book begins with an engaging introduction that sets the tone for the reader's journey. Drake's emphasis on the art and grace of rowing, rather than just the physical exertion, is refreshing and inspiring. He makes a compelling case for why indoor rowing, when done correctly, can be a life-long, sustainable activity that harmonizes mind, body, and spirit.

One of the standout features of this book is its structured approach. Divided into clear, logical sections, *Rowing from the Inside Out* covers everything from the basics of the rowing stroke to advanced techniques and the integration of the Alexander Technique and Tai Chi principles. Each chapter builds on the previous one, ensuring that readers develop a solid foundation before moving on to more complex concepts.

Drake's writing is both accessible and engaging. He skilfully explains technical aspects of rowing in a way that is easy to understand without oversimplifying. The inclusion of step-by-step instructions, supported by high-quality illustrations and video links, makes learning both visual and interactive. This multi-modal approach is particularly beneficial for those who may struggle with traditional text-based instruction.

The book also shines in its practical advice and tips for avoiding common mistakes and preventing injury. Drake's focus on intention, awareness, and understanding the mechanics of on-the-water rowing translates beautifully to the indoor rower. His insights into how the body should move and the importance of posture and balance are invaluable, making this book not just about rowing but about improving overall physical well-being.

Arianne Hoppler
Sculler at Yare Boat Club, Learning and Development Consultant and Yoga teacher

Acknowledgements

This book is the culmination of many influences over the years, including Alexander Technique (AT) teachers Patrick MacDonald, Misha Magidov and Marjory Barlow; and my Tai-chi teacher, Jim Uglow, for immersing me in the ocean of Tai-chi, although I have not left the lagoons. Without Patrick Pearson, I would probably have never discovered rowing.

Malcolm Balk, in observing me on the rowing machine one day, gave me the ah-ha! moment of realising the role of the pelvis in the release, helping me thereby to integrate ideas from AT and Tai-chi into rowing.

I would also like to thank all those generous souls at the Yare Boat Club, Norwich, UK, who tried to induct me into the art of sculling. Sadly time ran out to correspond with Frank Cunningham when this book was just the vaguest idea. Without him and Hugh Lade, who was coach at Lake Washington Rowing Club, my sense of what constitutes an ideal rowing action, would never have been sharpened.

On the way, various folks had faith that the project was worth it. They included Rebecca Caroe – now of *Rowing Chat*, who published the prelude to the book, *Rowing from a Holistic Perspective* – and Jackie Stanger and Bernd Dahlhaus. As a result this larger project was never entirely shelved.

The majority of the photographs and video clips were taken by my son, Leead Dereh Drake, who patiently saw me through my struggles to represent the key elements of rowing as I see them. I took the background cover photo and the one of Emma O'Reilly, who kindly modelled the indoor rowing picture on the front cover. Kim Hutchins introduced me to Kaarin Wall whose initial designs for the book inspired me to complete it.

And finally, I am so grateful to my wife, Angela, companion on our sculling venture on *Dude, Row-on-Air's* inflatable board, on the Norfolk Broads, who steered the editing process through to the final manuscript. Remarkably, we are still together!

Contents

Introduction

The art of it has always interested me more than the agony and the effort and all that.

Frank Cunningham, on receiving the highest honour of US Rowing in 2011

Do you aspire to row well, and with grace and power? Do you want to enjoy the experience of the rowing action itself, so that your rowing can become a sustainable, life-long activity?

You may be a beginner, or perhaps you already know something – even a good deal – about rowing. Because the rowing stroke is repeated, it is vital to cultivate good technique. This will reduce your risk of injury and improve performance, whether you want to row competitively or because you would like to maximise the health benefits of rowing.

The book's focus – and the starting point for many – is indoor rowing.

An extra dimension to this book is to explain fully *why* you might need to do certain things on the machine which is, after all, a rowing simulator. Would your movement on the indoor rower work on water? If so, you are more on likely to be the right lines.

And, making the transition to rowing in a boat will be a great deal easier if you've mastered good technique on the rowing machine. You will not have to *unlearn* movement patterns which could get in the way of acquiring the skills of rowing a boat efficiently through water.

Now if your gym or health club only contained one piece of equipment – and using it had to tick all the fitness boxes – what would it be? The answer is – you've guessed it – the indoor rower!

But how much of its potential is realised?

Through all the noise and disturbance in the gym environment, the characteristic timing of *whoosh, click, click, click, click, click* of the Concept 2 rower – used properly – is rarely heard. That sound might indicate that the rower has been in a racing shell and knows something about the rhythm and flow of the stroke. Another feature that is rarely seen is the swing of the body through the stroke, characteristic of the on-the-water rower.

More often however, rowing machines lie idle. The Cinderella of the gym. Occasionally one might be used for a few minutes as part of a cardiovascular workout. Little thought is given as to *how* to row. If it's just used for a short time much harm is unlikely to be caused, but all the benefits of rowing well won't be realised. Fitness instructors may have a sports science degree, but this does not usually include any training in rowing technique.

I recall an advert promoting a local gym. It showed a client sitting in a state of collapse towards the back of the rowing machine and next to him – clutching a clipboard – the instructor hunched in a squat. Both are smiling, apparently oblivious to what they are doing, the object of their attention being the numbers on the monitor. The instructor's advice might be something along the lines of "keep your back straight and row at 30 strokes a minute" (a racing speed!).

Some gym-goers do row for longer, but they treat the exercise as if they and the machine needed beating up; in so doing, what kind of "fitness" is being acquired? In extreme cases, they row in an almost demented fashion, showing the many possible ways in which a racing shell's movement through water would be sabotaged.

So what are the main benefits of using the indoor rower to its full potential? Improvements can be expected in your:

- Flexibility.
- Muscle tone throughout the body, including core strength and back stability.
- Endurance and cardio-vascular fitness.

The most important bonus, though – in understanding what an ideal rowing action entails – is that you can apply this coordination to moving better in everyday life.

- If you are normally *sat* for most of the day at work, you can find out how to *sit* better, more actively.

- You will also discover how to bend and lift in a more effective way.
- And your self-confidence will develop as you recover more poise, balance, and better posture.

Rowing has the image of being a gruelling, somewhat masochistic sport. It can, however, be a form of re-creation where mind, body and spirit can be harmonised in activity. Hence the title, *Rowing from the Inside Out*.

You may discover – if you have not done so already – that the experience of rowing can be deeply pleasurable. If it feels good you are more likely to return to it again and again, taking pleasure in developing your skills and celebrating your growing sense of mastery in movement.

I draw on ideas from two movement disciplines which – applied to rowing – will enhance your understanding of how to row with more ease and with less wasted, stressful effort.

The *Alexander Technique* is to do with improving postural awareness and the coordination of the whole body in everyday movement.

From *Tai-chi* you can learn how energy flows in your body and how to develop power, which is not just the exertion of muscular strength.

This book makes some novel suggestions on how best to integrate the rowing action:

- *Discover the sequence of changes in pressure on your feet*, which underpins the order of the body movements in the rowing stroke. Differences in physique will determine how much each part contributes to the whole and its precise timing through the drive. In the end, the rowing action is to be experienced as a flow of energy through the whole body.
- *Find out how to move seamlessly from drive to recovery* without the main body motion being arrested. This skill, largely ignored in conventional rowing circles, was well demonstrated by New Zealander Robbie Manson in the single shell. He still holds the world record for the fastest 2K time, because – amongst other things – he consistently rated higher than his taller, stronger opponents.
- *Experience the role of the fingers* in rehearsing, to some degree, the control of the handles – and therefore the blades – in on-the-water rowing.
- *Finally, explore how breathing naturally takes care of itself* in the cycle of the "gathering" and elongation of the spine in the rowing stroke.

So if you are a novice, this book will help you sustain your indoor rowing as a life-long activity.

For rowers with some experience – either indoors, or in a boat – it can help you to think afresh and refine aspects of your technique, which will serve you better both off and on the water.

Videos accompanying the text, numbered, are indicated like this:

▶ **Video # 1 View at: www.youtube.com/rowingfromtheinsideout**

Chapter Overviews

Part 1

Chapter 1 On rowing and some influential rowers

- The story of rowing.
- Rowing v paddling. Rowing v sculling.
- Influential rowers: Ned Hanlan and the sliding seat; Steve Fairbairn, the "father of modern rowing", and Frank Cunningham, who carried forward the "Thames Waterman" style of rowing into the 21st century.

Chapter 2 The rowing stroke – primer

- Aspects of the rowing stroke and its division into parts: two phases, the drive and recovery; and two transitions, entry/catch/connection and release. The metaphor of nature's seasons.
- The rowing stroke sequence illustrated by world record holder singles sculler, Robbie Manson.

Chapter 3 Those infernal machines

- Rowers' relationship with the rowing machine.
- Compare rowing machines: the nature of the resistance and "static" v "dynamic" machines and price.
- The *Concept 2* v the *WaterRower*, ergonomics, "feel" and aesthetics.
- The not-too-quick start guide: simple pointers to get started rowing.

Part 2

Chapter 4 User's manual

- Your body, how it functions in movement and how the mind influences patterns of movement: the relevance of the Alexander technique (AT).
- *The guiding insight that rowing is a bending and lifting action.*

- 10 mind-body explorations: "active" sitting, from stand to sit and sit to stand, location of the head-neck joint, range of motion at the head-neck joint, mapping the hip joints, allowing more space in the hip joints, hinging from the hips, pelvic rock and body swing, the role of the "lats" and "hanging off the handles".

Chapter 5 Warming up

- Monitor how the mind-body is responding to rowing at a low stroke rate. If undue stress and tension, lie down in the AT releasing position, described in detail.
- Mindful dynamic stretching to lubricate the joints, easing in to a moderate range of motion – Tai-chi-inspired movements to help with balance and symmetry.

Part 3

Chapter 6 Moving up the slide

- How to practise constructively: checking body use and focussing awareness.
- Unpicking the rowing action and building it in stages:

  - from arms and shoulders only, to pelvic rock and body swing, to quarter-slide, half-slide, three-quarters slide to full slide.

  - the three "halves" of the rowing stroke.

Chapter 7 The whole stroke...and nothing but

- Frank Cunningham's description of the whole stroke as a "unitary surge of energy".
- The circuit of energy described from a Taoist perspective.
- The basic sequence in the feet, described for the first time in this way.
- Visualise sculling oars as an extension of the arms. The importance of a relaxed hold in allowing the blades to slice into the water and to square quickly.
- The fundamental connections: from the *inside* of the heels to handle(s) to hips; from heels to handle(s) to hips to back, and from heels to handle(s) to hips to back to shoulders to arms.

- Ratio of the drive to the recovery and rhythm.
- How best to coordinate breathing?
- Meditate on the breath.
- Rowing as meditation.

Chapter 8 The no-sweat rowing workout

- A cautionary tale of going too hard, too soon.
- The value of using a heart monitor.
- Starting out: "pyramid" workouts.

Chapter 9 Cooling down and stretching

- Why stretch?
- Range of motion stretches for hamstrings and calves – superficial and deep.
- After rowing, restoring range of motion: static stretches for the spine, shoulders, forearms and fingers, quads and glutes.

Part 4

Chapter 10 Alexander technique and the sport of rowing

- Are injuries to competitive rowers largely preventable?
- The Oxford and Cambridge Boat Race: FM Alexander's commentary on stresses shown by rowers.
- The application of AT to two of the athletes competing in the Athens Olympics of 2004.
- The author's unpublished letter: observations of one athlete's injury woes prior to the 2012 Olympics.
- An AT teacher's ground-breaking work with German, Swiss and Austrian elite rowers.

Chapter 11 Beyond indoor rowing

- The author's experience of becoming a recreational sculler late in life.
- Three less well-known sculling drills from Cunningham.
- A short introduction to other forms of whole body exercise: walking and running, skating, swimming and Tai-chi.

PART 1

1

On rowing and some influential rowers

Row, row, row your boat
Gently down the stream
Merrily, merrily, merrily, merrily
Life is but a dream.

On Rowing

Understanding a little of the story of rowing, and some of its most inspiring figures, will help you to appreciate how the main features of rowing action have evolved, and why I take most inspiration from a particular tradition of rowing style[1].

Rowing has its roots in antiquity, with the Egyptians, Greeks, and Romans. Originally it was employed in warfare and in transport but, as far back as 2000 years ago, races were held to keep crews fit, as well as for sport and entertainment. Before the arrival of mechanised boats, fishing boats and lifeboats were propelled by oars – and were often crewed by men who could not swim!

The *Thames Watermen* and their rowing boats were the water taxis of the Middle Ages, when there were few bridges. Transporting passengers was hard labour and paid well if you were quick. The fastest watermen participated in the world's oldest rowing race, the prize being the *Dogget* (an ornamental coat) and a Badge.

The upper classes, who went to the universities of Cambridge and Oxford, saw rowing as a gentlemanly sport. They thought they knew how to row and were instrumental in forming the Amateur Rowing Association. For many years they excluded the artisan rowers from the lower classes, such as the Thames Watermen, from competing in regattas.

Rowing v paddling

Paddling is often confused with *rowing* although, when rowers talk of paddling, they mean to row "lightly or casually".

In canoeing and kayaking paddles are used, by one or more forward-facing persons, to *pull* the boat forward with their paddles. The legs have a role, but a minor one; and the boat travels with a slight zig-zag motion.

In rowing, one or more rowers face *backward*. This is one of the paradoxes of rowing, allowing the levering of the boat *forward* by means of oars; placed in oarlocks or rowlocks, these act as fulcra. Perhaps this is a metaphor for life: you can know what has passed, but you only get to glimpse, uncertainly, what is coming!

In a wider rowing boat or "wherry", with a fixed seat, the upper body provides the work for propulsion.

In the narrow racing shell – slim, long and light, to cut through the water – there is a sliding seat; power is generated mainly by pushing with the legs, although the back comes strongly into play next; and finally, the oars are pulled through using shoulders and arms. If one oar is resting flat on the water, rowing with the other would draw the boat in circles.

Both sports have now developed indoor simulators to mimic the body actions of paddlers and rowers on the water.

Rowing v Sculling

To maximise speed, stability is sacrificed by making the hull narrow – not much wider than the rower's hips. And helping the boat ride high, to minimise drag, it is now made of carbon fibre. A single scull weighs just over 30lb (14kg) and is a little over 26' (8m) long. Balance is maintained by keeping the oars roughly level – placed in oarlocks with outriggers, which swivel – attached to the sides of the boat.

The term "rowing" is applied to:

- **Rowing**, where one (longer) sweep oar is used by each rower.
- **Sculling**, where each sculler uses a pair of oars.

At least two rowers – a "pair" – are needed to balance the boat with *sweep oar*. This is the trickiest, but potentially the most satisfying, rowing partnership. From then on, up to four or eight rowers are involved, and most university rowing consists of these crews. With these larger crew boats the coxswain or cox steers, guides, and motivates the rowers.

Sculling crews normally number two (a "double") or four (a "quad"), and each sculler has two oars – slightly shorter than sweep oars – to balance the boat. Unusually, there might be three, or even eight, scullers in a boat. Sculling boats with the same number of oarsmen will generally go faster than the equivalent number of rowers: two oars are more efficient than one. Sculling's great merit is that it's possible to scull solo in a single shell.

Some influential rowers

Of those who have made significant contributions, to the development of rowing style over the years, three key individuals are highlighted here, dating from the late 19C to the start of the millennium.

They thought deeply about how to make boats go faster and all were passionate about the flow and beauty of the rowing stroke, performed well. They continue to inspire rowers to this day.

Ned Hanlan (1855–1908) [2]

His contemporaries said of Ned Hanlan that he was the finest sculler they had ever seen. The son of Irish immigrants, who ran a hotel on Toronto Island in Canada, Hanlan spent much of his childhood "messing about in boats". From the age of five, rowing himself to the mainland to attend school must have developed a natural feel for the water. By the age of 16 he was competing in races, and from 1880–1884 he was the sculling world champion.

It is hard now to appreciate the extent of his achievement, and just how much interest there was in rowing at the time. As many as a hundred-thousand spectators would line up on riverbanks or follow in steamboats – the kind of mass participation seen at football matches or popular music events today.

Huge sums of money were placed on bets, and Hanlan became wealthy through his racing.

People wondered how such a slight man – only 5'9" (175cm) and around 150lbs (68kg) – could be so successful against much bigger opponents. One factor – as well as the swivelling gates attached to the oarlocks which lengthened his stroke – was that he was the first sculler to fully exploit the use of the *sliding seat*. Previously, rowers used greased leather pads to slide a little, a blistering experience. The sliding seat was developed in the early 1870s and Hanlan experimented with longer and longer slides. This enabled much more power to be generated through the legs and hips.

No film record exists from which to analyse his form. What commentators at the time remarked on was how seamless, integrated, and fluid his rowing action was, often at slower stroke rates (in the early 30s range) than his opponents. His boat appeared to move steadily through the water, as if being pulled continuously by a string. A contemporary newspaper account described his sculling:

> *There was a combination of grace and strength and the perfection of motion that appealed to the eye in the same way as the thoroughbred racehorse does.*

After his retirement, in 1897, he made an important statement about his sculling technique, which we will explore later:

> *It came across my mind like a flash that the control of the whole motion of the body while in the boat lay in my feet.*

He had noticed his tendency to lunge forward onto his feet, before reaching "catch" – the beginning of the drive – which tended to slow his boat down. It took him some time to change this habit:

> *... and by degree got every muscle in my body working in perfect unison.*

Another factor, in checking the speed of the boat, was the delay between the end of the "drive" (the power phase of the stroke) and the beginning of the "recovery" (the release phase). To minimise that, he developed a pendular swing of his body at this transition. To an observer, it was hard to see the ending of the *swing back* and the beginning of the *swing forward.* By reducing the amount of time with his body weight towards the bow, the boat rode higher in the water and cut through it more effectively. His overall conclusion was:

> *...mere endurance and brute strength do not make the successful oarsman... the man must use his head as well as his physical gifts.*

These pointers influence this book's approach to the rowing stroke. Hanlan was the supreme sculler, but the coaching career that followed the end of his racing days was not as successful as that of his rivals.

Steve Fairbairn (1862–1938)

Steve Fairbairn is known as the "father of modern rowing". Not quite in the top ranks as a rower, he was, however, unparalleled in his career as *the* philosopher-coach. Most of the questions about how to row well – which coaches still wrestle with today – Fairbairn debated exhaustively. The merits and demerits of his arguments even made the front pages of major newspapers.

From an Australian farming family of Scottish descent, he was a talented all-round athlete and sportsman, skilled in rugby and football, gymnastics and field athletics, swimming, and of course, rowing.

He attended Jesus College, Cambridge (1881-87) and soon made his mark on the rowing scene, both as oarsman and coach. There is no evidence that he witnessed Hanlan sculling, but it's hard to believe he would not have taken the opportunity to do so – the Canadian, attracting so much attention, must have influenced him.

Fairbairn, too, exploited the potential of the new sliding seat. He reacted strongly

against the prevailing English Orthodox style of rowing, promoted by the gentleman rowers at Oxbridge. They emphasized a "correct" – and rather stiff – militaristic posture, through the extreme forward and backward swings that the stroke demanded. The extra leg action that the sliding seat afforded was only grafted on to the same use of the back and arms as with a fixed seat. Body movement came first, legs finished the drive.

Fairbairn taught his crews to concentrate on "working the oars", rather than thinking about what the body should do; according to him, rowing technique had no purpose other than to make the boat move faster.

When he returned to Jesus College, Cambridge, in 1903, he discovered that much of what he had taught previously had, in the meantime, been supplanted by the orthodoxy that he had tried to overturn. Later he also coached at the Thames and London Rowing Clubs.

Starting in 1904, four volumes of material – as well as copious correspondence – were published over the next thirty years or so, railing against English Orthodox Rowing and setting down his philosophy of the sport[3].

He wanted oarsmen to "think for themselves". He encouraged them to read and meditate on his notes on rowing before retiring to bed. He created seasonal training programmes, similar to the kind of preparation serious competitive rowers follow today. "Mileage creates champions" was one of his maxims – and this still applies.

Fairbairn created "Head of the River" races, which most club rowers are now familiar with: one boat goes off after another for approximately twice the distance of racing in parallel on the wide waterways of the standard international 2K distance.

Over the years, he changed his mind on many things. For instance, he maintained that "the body should be held firmly braced, taut, elastic and whalebony; and not allowed to sit floppily or loose". He also wrote that "to move the body correctly, the body must move unconsciously"; and that "being body conscious" was the first step towards what he named "locomotor ataxia" (the inability to control movement, which becomes jerky and uncoordinated).

The year after Fairbairn returned to London, Frederick Matthias Alexander arrived from Australia. As far as is known, they did not meet.

Alexander was in London to promote his technique for improving overall mind-body coordination. In contrast to Fairbairn, whose primary objective was the manipulation of oars in order to row faster, Alexander's concern was more universal: how is it possible to coordinate any movement in any situation?

At that stage, he did not make observations on the sport of rowing; these came later, as described in Chapter 10.

Frank Cunningham (1922–2013)

American Frank Cunningham was "stroke" (leading rower) for the Harvard Eight's success against Yale in 1947, breaking the world record. He began coaching the following year, drawing on the time-honed skills of the Thames Watermen – who provided the original taxi service on London's waterway. His main influences were the English professional sculler, Bert Haines, at Harvard; and George Pocock.

Cunningham became coach at Lake Washington Rowing Club (LWRC) in Seattle, in 1980. He taught high school English for over 30 years, and his facility with language and clarity of thought made *The Sculler at Ease* (first published in 1992)[4] the classic exposition on sculling as an art.

In 2010, on receiving the highest honour that American rowing can bestow, he mused on the passion that seemed to drive him year after year:

> If I'm upset with one of my students, I will say that they are turning art into exercise...And I think the people who get the most out of the sport go at it as a lifetime pursuit of excellence, of getting it right.
>
> The art of it has always interested me more than the agony and the effort and all that...I always tell people that if they want to understand athleticism – and see it in its purest form – go to the zoo. All of the animals are athletes. If you're talking about skill and grace versus awkwardness or clumsiness, all the clumsy animals are dead.
>
> Grace is what allows the species to prevail. We have an innate sense of grace, but it has to be fostered.

At LWRC he worked with scullers of all levels of ability, up to Olympians John Bigelow and Paul Enquist in 1984, as well as Sherri Cassuto in 1988.

Concerned that the old Thames Waterman style of rowing she'd learnt from him could be lost, Cassuto recorded it on video for posterity[5]. She did not know of anyone who rowed in this way who had suffered back injury. As a scientist, comparing conventional methods of rowing with the Thames Waterman style, she also maintained that what she'd learnt from Cunningham made her scull faster in a single shell; yet, in a crew boat, she was able to switch to rowing in the same way – the approved American style of the day – as the others.

Before exploring the depths of the rowing action, the basics are introduced next.

2

The Rowing Stroke: primer

The perfect stroke is a perfect gesture:
seamless, spontaneous and graceful.

Frank Cunningham

The most obvious flaws, in most gym goers' use of the rowing machine, are poor rhythm and absence of body swing. It seems clear that they have had no experience of rowing on water, nor viewed film of rowers in action to figure out proper technique – although the C-shaped spine is highly problematic in many elite rowers.

The vision of the perfectly integrated stroke that Cunningham experienced – and tried to convey to his students – is the guiding principle. *But where to start?* What are the component parts of the rowing stroke? And how do they fit together?

The parts of the rowing stroke

The two main parts – or phases – of the rowing stroke are the DRIVE and the RECOVERY. Most users of indoor rowers mix up the two. They tend to rush the slide on the way forward – still working hard – and they do not allow the body to recover from the effort of the drive.

As a consequence, with the body not poised at the beginning of the stroke, the drive is less effective. No wonder gym users don't spend long on the indoor rower – it can't be very satisfying – and yet, better use of the rowing machine has so much unrealised potential.

The drive, the power phase of the stroke, is when work is applied to move the boat through the water, or – on the indoor rowing machine – to overcome resistance by moving paddles through water, or air through a flywheel.

The recovery entails gliding into position – ready for the next stroke – by expending the least amount of energy, and by relaxing muscles that have contracted during the drive.

The transition from *drive* to *recovery* is called the RELEASE; and from *recovery* to *drive* it is called CATCH or CONNECTION, when the body is primed to start the stroke.

The whole rowing stroke can now be previewed by looking at snapshots of the world's fastest sculler, the Kiwi Robbie Manson, in action.

As far as the essentials of his main body movement are concerned, he exemplifies a beautiful style of rowing, well worth studying and emulating, even if the reader may never venture out in a boat.

Watch Manson's world record-breaking race at Poznan, Poland, in 2017 on You tube[1]; everything came together on that day.

To view go to:

https://www.youtube.com/watch?v=plXhvUJoVMY&t=281s

At 4 minutes 25 seconds in, he is shown in close up: play it in slow motion. Many of the features of good body movement during the rowing stroke can be observed.

Here is the basic sequence of the rowing stroke, to be explored in detail later:

Manson's world record-breaking race at Poznan, Poland, in 2017

Connection / catch
ready to spring off the stretcher

Drive beginning
hips and handles moving together

Mid-drive
back opening up

End-drive
shoulders drawing in the arms

The rowing cycle – the ongoing renewal of the whole stroke – could be compared to the seasons of the year. Craig Lambert in *Mind over Water: lessons in life from the art of rowing,* observes that the stroke cycle and the life cycle are one. Experience all the seasons in two or three seconds!

The *drive* and *recovery* are, then, the high seasons of the year, summer and winter.

The transitional seasons, spring and autumn, represent change of direction at each end of the stroke.

Spring, when the rower "springs" off the foot stretcher and the sap rises, is the culmination of all the subtle changes that take place through winter, as when plants put their energies into laying down roots. The CATCH is that moment in the rowing stroke where the body, gathering itself to generate as much power as possible, can be quiet in its entirety.

If you look for this transition on video of a competitive rower going hard, and rating very high, you might find yourself doing a "double take" because, however fast the overall movement, the rower appears motionless at that point.

The "catch" in on-water rowing is sometimes called "entry". The equivalent for the indoor rower can be named "CONNECTION", implying that all parts of the body are ready to work together – and yet in opposition to each other – as you'll come to see. The drive – or **Summer** phase – is when the blades of the oars, submerged, prise the boat through the water. ▸

Release
follow through from drive to recovery

Recovery
body swings forwards, sending handles away

Quarter slide
hands beyond knees, which now bend

Half slide
body achieves the same angle as at full slide

Recovery ended
poised at full slide, ready to go again!

◀ Towards the end of the drive, the **Fall** or **Autumn** of the stroke is when the blades are released from the water. This is often called the "finish" in the boat, which puts in mind the idea of a separation between drive and "recovery".

Instead, think of the ending of the drive following straight through into the recovery without pause – a continuous motion of body and arms. Fairbairn called the whole stroke an "endless chain". Here, the term "RELEASE" works well for both the boat and the indoor rower.

Then there's a return to **Winter**, the RECOVERY phase, when the boat continues its glide underneath the rower. On the indoor machine, you'll rely on the rocking-over of the body from the pelvis, and the activation of the hamstrings (the muscles at the back of the thighs), to generate easy movement up the slide. As if a tree has to drive its roots deep into the earth by the end of winter, the rower must wait until the very last moment before transferring their weight onto the foot stretcher to spring off at the beginning of the drive. And the cycle starts again.

In the next chapter, rowing machines, how they work and their relative merits, will be discussed.

3

Those Infernal Machines

Rowers have a love-hate relationship with the rowing machine ... they would rather be on the water, enjoying the stimulation of the outdoors, their senses alive to the instability of the boat and changing conditions.

The rowing machine, however, does not have to be entirely second-best to the boat. It can be a portal to the world of on the water. I started out on the indoor rower, using it regularly for a couple of years before learning to scull. You could view indoor and outdoor rowing as a to-and-fro experience, the one enriching the other. The rowing machine can serve as a laboratory for you to experiment with the main body movements needed in the boat, as well as a great way for anyone to discover and enjoy rowing.

The rowing machine's common name in rowing circles is the *ergo* in Britain and the *erg* elsewhere, abbreviated from *ergometer* – which means a machine for measuring work or energy expended. One individual's performance can be compared against another on the same make of machine. Nonetheless, rowing coaches know that "pulling a good score" on the erg does not necessarily translate into what a rower can achieve in the boat.

The work that is being done on the ergometer is, of course, to row. How well do rowing machines simulate the experience of rowing in a boat? And how do the different kinds compare?

The main criteria to be considered are whether:

- The seat slides on its own, or whether the main part of the indoor rower moves as well.
- Resistance is hydraulic, magnetic, air or water.
- Some instability is allowed, as on water.

- The ergonomics of the indoor rower are directly comparable to the boat: for example, seat height in relation to foot stretcher, and the separation of the feet.

One of the first indoor rowers to be manufactured was designed in 1900 and worked on hydraulic resistance. It was included in the gym of the ill-fated Titanic.

The current generation of indoor rowers really started with the *Concept* rowing machine. Utilising air resistance, it became available in the early 1980s, followed by the *WaterRower,* later that decade. These rowers are so-called "static" rowing machines**:** the seat moves but the rest of the machine is stationary.

Since then, attempts have been made to simulate more closely the experience of being in a boat. First came "dynamic" rowing machines, the main body of the equipment moving underneath the rower, as well as the seat. Of these, the cheapest (double the price of the basic Concept 2 or WaterRower) is the *Oartex DX* and the *RP3* from *RowPerfect* (nearly 3x the price). These are prized by competitive rowers for replicating the body movement in a racing shell and are said to reduce the loading on joints that some static machines can cause.

RowPerfect is increasingly being used by national rowing federations as the standard machine to compare rowing performance between athletes. Like the *Concept 2*, they both use air resistance, but are even noisier in the home environment. And the size and price of dynamic rowers mean they are less appealing to the home user. More recently, Concept 2 have developed a dynamic rowing machine (costing half as much again as their basic model) where most of the movement is in the foot stretcher.

At an even bigger premium – about 5x the cost of the brand leaders of static machines – are the rowing "simulators", such as the *SimulatOar* from the Coffey Corporation and the *Biorower*. One big advantage is they can be used with two handles – or one – to mimic sculling or sweep oar; and the handles can easily be rotated to practise feathering and squaring the blades. Apart from cost, the main drawback is they take up even more space – especially widthways – to accommodate the oar handles. The *Biorower* is a brilliant state-of-the-art, cleverly thought-through piece of engineering, but is unlikely to take its place in most people's living rooms anytime soon.

At the other end of the scale, it is possible to buy rowing machines for as little as £/$100 or less. However, they will not feel so good – nor be as durable – as the two I suggest should be top your list for serious consideration: the *Concept 2* and the *WaterRower* (and its various imitations), which cost around £/$ 1000.

As a footnote, should you fall out of love with indoor rowing (hard to believe!) and want to sell your machine, you would not be much out of pocket: they hold good value in the second-hand market.

The most recent machine aimed at the gym market, the *Technogym Skillrow*, uses both air and magnetic resistance. It is a bulky piece of equipment and costs almost four times as much as the *Concept 2*. If I had the space and the cash, the rowing simulators mentioned previously would win hands down.

The Concept 2

This is *the* machine associated with indoor rowing, available in the majority of gyms. Most competitive rowers have served time on this machine. Developed by Olympic rowing brothers, Dick and Pete Dreissigacker, it was the first mass-market and all-time best-selling rowing machine: reliable, durable, well-built, it became the one used to compare rowing performance on land and at indoor rowing competitions.

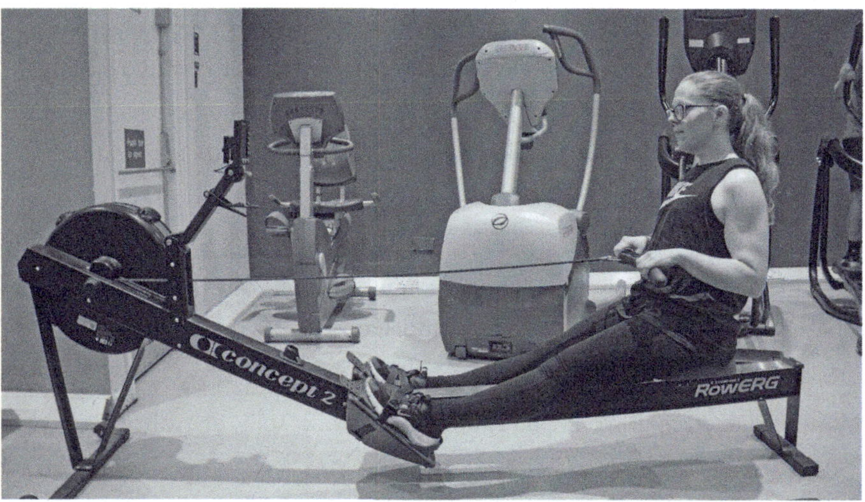

The current incarnation, the *Concept 2 Model E*, has gone through some modifications over the years. The *Model D* is the standard machine; the main feature of the *Model E*, apart from increased cost, is that the seat is higher off the floor, so it's easier to get on and off for someone with restricted mobility.

Concept 2s use air resistance. They are not as noisy as the dynamic rowers, but the movement of the chain produces a rasping sound, even on well-maintained machines. And I must confess to having some antipathy to feeling "enchained".

Adjustment

You can readily alter the resistance of the machine by means of the "damper" lever at the side of the machine. Gym users routinely set the damper to its maximum of 10, thinking that a heavier work-out is better. It is more likely that they will risk injury. The extra loading will tend to over-work the upper body – and at the wrong point in the rowing stroke.

It is worth checking out the *actual* resistance on one of these machines at the gym. If they are not well maintained, dust builds up in the mechanism and affects the resistance. To work within the resistance of being in a boat – roughly 1-3 on a well-maintained machine – you might have to set the damper lever to, for example, 5-7 on another machine. Here's how to check:

The Concept 2's PM5 performance monitor

Follow the main menu:

- *> Select other options > display drag factor > row to display drag factor.*
- Then, simply row.
- After a few strokes you will see a number appearing in the window of the monitor.
- Adjust the damper lever until you see 110-120, roughly the resistance of rowing in a single scull.

You will find there are lots of options within the *PM5*. As well as being able to view, in real time, the distance, length of time and how many strokes per minute (spm) are rowed, you can also see how much energy has been expended, either in calories or watts.

More advanced features include monitoring your "split" and displaying your "force curve":

- The split lets you know how much time it will take for you to row 500m at your current pace.
- The force curve shows you how much force is being applied all the way through the drive. An ideal shape is close to an inverted U or parabola. It should look smooth, which implies a continuous application of force.

My main reservation about the *Concept 2* is to do with "feel"; it does not remotely feel like pulling oars in water. And there is a slight delay before the mechanism takes up at the beginning of the drive, which can impact the lower back.

Another *potential* drawback (which could be an advantage if you have flexibility issues) is that the seat is set higher (even on the *Model D*) – and the feet are placed wider apart – than in the boat. The ergonomics of indoor rower and boat would ideally be equivalent if you wanted to move from the indoor rower onto the water, so that stiffness can be identified and addressed in advance.

Perhaps serious rowers just opt for the *Concept 2* out of habit and availability. It is what most rowers drawn to competition have always used, are still using and will probably continue to use for the foreseeable future.

Finally, a minor plus of the *Concept 2* is that you can row barefoot, helping you to really sense your connection to the foot stretcher through your feet.

Note that the foot stretcher of the *WaterRower* – up for consideration next – can create uncomfortable pressure just above the heels if you are barefoot. To avoid this, wear shoes to protect your feet – but of the barefoot ("minimal") kind.

The WaterRower

Following on from the *Concept 2*, the *WaterRower*, developed by another rower, John Duke, appeared in 1988. It won design awards: it looks beautiful and although some plastic and metal are used in its construction, first impressions are simply of wood and water (in a clear tank). A big advantage in the home environment is that it can be wheeled upright and stored against a wall, taking up no more floor space than a large dining chair.

The main aspect of its appeal, apart from its appearance, is that it feels and sounds great.

In use, the water, driven by a paddle flywheel, makes a soft *whooshing* sound. And, although the dynamic and simulator rowers replicate some aspects of the rowing experience better, it is hard to beat the organic feel of water resistance. Connection at the beginning of the drive starts smoothly and can be sustained all the way through.

Resistance *can* be altered by the amount of water in the tank, but you are not able quickly or substantially to change it, unlike the Concept 2. However, the

recommended water levels produce a resistance close to the amount of work in a single scull; and the harder you row, the more resistance increases.

The ergonomics of the *WaterRower* are more similar to that of a boat than the *Concept 2*, the feet being closer together on the foot stretcher and the seat set lower. So, your main body movement translates more directly from indoor to outdoor rowing, but the machine is less forgiving if you are stiff. You could view this as an impediment or, alternatively, as an opportunity to address any flexibility issues. In the short run, you could place an extra firm pad on the seat to raise you a little and make it easier on the hamstrings.

The WaterRower's S4 performance monitor

The *S4* monitor offers a similar range of performance indicators to the *Concept 2's*. The monitor is low and slightly offset to the right, so you can gaze into the distance without having the monitor "in your face", yet the display is big enough to glance at the information when needed.

The home screen enables you to see your current speed in meters per second, but this can be changed to meters or miles per hour if you wish. There is more delay in registering changes of pace on the display than with the *Concept 2*.

Summary

Whichever machine you choose, the rowing action across all machines should be essentially the same. On all indoor rowers you can adjust the position of your feet on the foot stretcher.

If your overriding aim is to compete with other rowers – most of whom will be using *Concept 2s* – then your choice is made.

Although I have had access to the *Concept 2* at my local gym, the *WaterRower* is the machine I choose to use at home. For me, it wins hands down for "feel". As you row, the sound of water whooshing in the tank is meditative and calming.

The not-too-quick start guide

OK, so by now you are probably desperate to start rowing! You know, of course, there's much more to discover, but what are the main points to be considered when you just want to have a go?

Preliminaries: you, the machine ... and the music?

- First, **how are you feeling**? If stressed, unduly tired or in discomfort or pain, the best thing to do is to lie down for a few minutes in the Alexander Technique releasing position (see chapter 5), your head supported in a neutral position on soft-back books, knees bent and feet flat. If that improves matters, set up the rower:
- **Adjust the resistance of the machine**. If you are using a Concept 2 indoor rower, move the damper lever to between 2 – 4, roughly the resistance you would encounter in a single scull. Move the foot stretcher until it's a comfortable height for you.
- Pay attention to yourself and how you are rowing, especially if there's music playing in the gym.

Rowing

▶ **Video # 1 View at: www.youtube.com/rowingfromtheinsideout**

1 To take your seat on the rower, hinge forwards from the hips before allowing the knees to bend.

2 Place your feet on the foot stretcher and leave the straps loose. Keep your feet in contact with the foot stretcher throughout the drive phase.

3 With legs straight, but knees soft, sitting towards the back of the machine, explore swinging a little back and forwards from the hips without bending your knees.

4 The next time on the forward swing, let the knees bend passively and allow the seat to slide forwards.

5 Stop moving forwards when your heels begin to lighten on the foot stretcher. How tall can you sit, even while leaning forwards a little?

6 Lightly hold the handle with the ends of your fingers.

7 Rowing with the sliding seat is a leg-dominant action. Start the drive from the legs – off the flat of the feet – followed by the body opening; finish the drive by drawing the shoulders back to "reel" the arms in. The hands arrive close to the lower ribs.

8 As the body starts swinging forwards again on the recovery, send the handle slightly downwards and away.

9 Only when the handle passes over your knees, do you allow them to bend.

10 Ease forwards without rushing: let the recovery phase last longer than the drive phase.

11 Row at a steady rate of between 18 – 22 spm (strokes per minute).

Enjoy!

Now we've looked at ergos and been on a machine, take time to explore, trouble-shoot and coordinate the kinds of movement needed in the rowing action – the subject of the next chapter.

PART 2

4

User's manual

All strenuous exercise will reinforce the existing co-ordination of the body – or the lack of it.

Patrick Macdonald, master teacher trainer of the Alexander Technique

Having been introduced to how rowing machines function, it's important to ask the question: *how do I work?*

How do your mind and body interact, to set up the best conditions for rowing?

It's not uncommon in rowing circles to hear of a coach instructing their athletes, "keep your posture!" However, such a statement lacks nuance and betrays a basic misunderstanding about the nature of "posture".

The use of the body necessarily needs to change dynamically in all activities, not least in rowing. So, even if an athlete achieves good "body use" at a particular moment, if they try to keep it – as though it was a position to be "held" – they will invariably stiffen and interfere with their breathing.

To row well, and to avoid injury, fundamental movement patterns – often taken for granted – will be explored, with help from the Alexander Technique (AT) and Tai-chi.

You'll come to an understanding of what Alexander called "the use of the self" – the whole mind-body in action.

Experiment with the following movement patterns on your own, or ideally with the guidance of an Alexander Teacher. These can become part of your everyday movement possibilities.

It is conceivable that you might be supremely well-coordinated and, if so, you *could* put this chapter aside, for the present. However, if you want to refine what you are doing on the indoor rower – or in a boat – take time to study this chapter.

This is especially important if you are already familiar with rowing; you might be in the groove – and little short of perfection – or you could, unknowingly, be compounding poor movement patterns, which become harder to change later.

It's helpful here to understand something of the **conscious competence learning model** of how psychophysical skills are acquired.

The starting point is to be open to finding out what you don't know about something you could do better. This is the "unconscious incompetence" stage, which can then proceed to "conscious incompetence": that is, when the things that aren't working so well come into view.

Then there is the possibility of change. This is what this chapter is all about.

And – you've guessed it – the next stage is "conscious competence", the subject of the next chapter, where the focus will be on unpicking and beginning to execute the various parts of the rowing action more effectively.

On the question of rowing technique, many rowers simply want to know what will make boats go *faster*. Their main concern comes down to the physical aspects of the sport. *How can I be stronger and fitter and pull harder?*

In the late 1990s, Alexander Teacher Gwen Dobie in Victoria BC, Canada, was consulted by elite Masters' sculler Val Thompson Williams, who felt she had hit a brick wall in her training. However strenuously she trained – up to six hours a day – Val was unable to go faster.

Gwen observed how muscle-bound Val was, and that the movement pattern required for rowing – squatting – caused Val to stiffen her neck and pull her head backwards and downwards:

> *"she was clamping downwards throughout her spine."*

Here is Val's account of the transformation – not only in her rowing, but also in her whole life – through having lessons in AT[1]:

> The Alexander Technique was useful firstly in providing the opportunity to understand and adopt the principle of "non-doing". Being a very driven individual, all of my interest and my way of being in the world was to "do" something. Hard and fast and well – always with the goal of bigger, faster, and stronger. And I carried all that "thought effort" around in my body. It was very clenched, tight and, I thought, strong.
>
> Over time, the Technique changed how I worked, my body, my thinking, my feelings and finally my whole life. I relaxed into my body, allowing it to work only when I wanted it to and not all the time. (It was used to working, even at rest.) I learned to allow my body, myself, my mind, my emotions, to be at rest. In that rest, in that non-doing, came information and knowledge and, ultimately, (a little?) wisdom...
>
> In sport specifically, my experience has been enhanced tenfold by the Alexander Technique. I would highly recommend it to any athlete. The ability to leave the body alone, to elicit its natural effort rather than trying to "do" something faster, longer, stronger, etc, was phenomenal. I found my ergometer and racing skills getting much quicker by trying to "not do". Having the luxury of a quantitative work environment (everything is timed and measured), and a specific daily AT focus, provided the immediate feedback that the Technique "worked". But I was quickly reminded again for the millionth time that AT is not the "end-all" to getting quicker.
>
> Remember, allowing no [unnecessary] work is the goal...just to be. It was a real boost to my mental training to have the Technique in my back pocket when I placed ninth in in the 1999 Canadian Women's Open Lightweight Erging Championships and when I rowed in the Masters' Nationals (5 gold) and World Lightweight Championships (2 gold) and the Royal Canadian Henley Regatta (1 gold). I spent a lot of my time in a single, the rest in a double. I was thrilled with my placings in these events. Besides training effectively, I can definitely say, without hesitation, that I wouldn't have had the rowing success that I have had the luxury of experiencing in my short time on the water, without finding AT and the great teachers that I have had the privilege to work with.

The Alexander Technique: FM's story

So, what *is* the Alexander Technique (AT) and how can it help anyone, particularly rowers?

It all began with the search by Australian actor, Frederick Matthias ("FM") Alexander (1869-1955), for a solution to the hoarseness that was increasingly marring his stage performances. Normal speech did not seem to present him with any difficulties, but, under the stress of delivering monologues, his voice tended to give out.

Doctors reassured him that there was no serious underlying pathology. When resting his voice did not cure the problem, they agreed that it must be something he was *doing* – when performing a speech – that was interfering with his voice. However, they had no idea what that could be. When asked what they had noticed of him, his acting colleagues remarked that his breathing was noisy – a sign of tension and restriction in his throat.

FM's inner journey

Alexander then determined to work out exactly what was going wrong. He placed himself in front of an arrangement of mirrors to see if there was difference between what he was doing while reciting, compared to normal speaking – which did not appear to create any difficulties.

At first, he could not identify anything. However, as his powers of observation grew, he began to observe certain postural tendencies which were actually present all the time – but which became more exaggerated under performance conditions.

A key element was his tendency to stiffen his neck and pull back his head during recitation – the same thing that many rowers do at the catch.

Later, he came to understand that the root of his problem was not simply what he *did*, but the preceding *idea,* or intention of reciting, which created the "Doing" that interfered with his voice.

He began teaching other actors about the "use of the self". As word spread, members of the public consulted him about their chronic health problems that had not been solved by doctors. A wide range of health symptoms seemed to be helped by improving the ways that they used themselves. Alexander began to see that he had stumbled upon something of far greater significance than simply improving vocal technique: a universal method of facilitating overall coordination, and consequently better functioning.

In *Evolution of a Technique* – the title of the main chapter in his book, *The Use of the Self*[2] –he documents his process of self-discovery, and the conclusions he came to. These conclusions form the basic ideas of AT, which will be drawn on extensively throughout this book:

- **Unity of mind and body.** Nothing can be understood fully in its separate parts, except in the context of the whole "mind-body" in action.
- **Force of habit and faulty body awareness.** The depth and range of "limiting patterns of coordination" should not be underestimated, nor the fact that it may be difficult, at first, to *sense* the "doing" which interferes with the desired outcome. And it follows that the changes that may be needed could feel unfamiliar and quite wrong at first.
- **"End-gaining" versus the "means-whereby".** How an individual strives, and often fails, to attain their goal directly. Choosing instead to put energy into the best means of achieving an end – and being prepared to forego quick results – is often the more effective and efficient method, in the long term.

- **"Thinking-in-activity".** To trust in the mind to come to a "condition of quiet", where harmful and habitual movement patterns can be let go of, and the body "invited" to organise itself in a better way. This involves a process of *giving directions,* which facilitate the *dynamic* relationship of neck to head to torso (including the pelvis), which in turn influences the coordination of the limbs. Alexander called this the *"primary control"*.

In their early years, most children naturally learn to stand, bend, walk and move around in all sorts of ways, with great facility. Now however, as people have become increasingly screen-bound from an early age and more sedentary than ever – compounded by the effects of various injuries and emotional factors – the ability to move well into their later years is often seriously compromised.

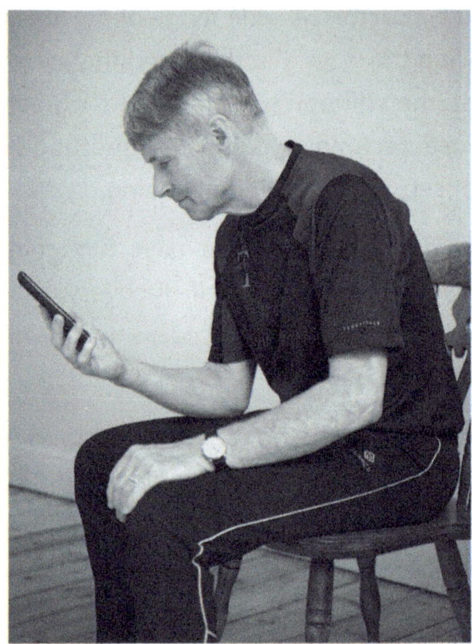

A modern malaise

What a joy to watch elite athletes and sports stars perform at the highest level; they make extraordinary feats look like a stroll in the park. So, what can be done to recover more ease of movement?

With Alexander's ideas in mind, and while clarifying some basic anatomical realities, the exploration can begin. Be prepared for some new, unfamiliar experiences which may feel strange at first, but your movement should come to feel easier and less effortful. Enjoy the adventure!

Rowing as a bending and lifting action: the key insights

Video # 2 View at: www.youtube.com/rowingfromtheinsideout

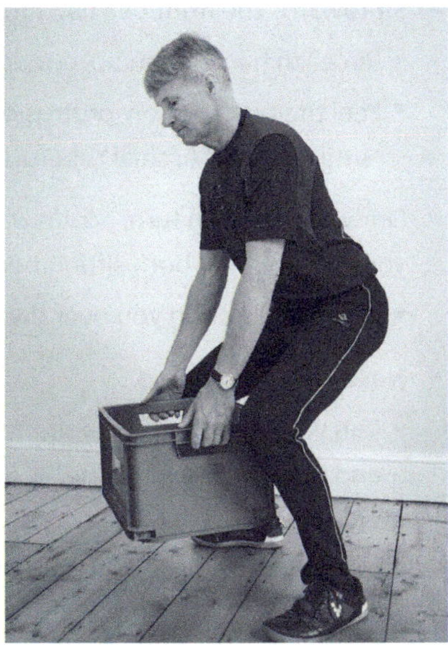

Rowing is essentially a bending and lifting action, performed in a horizontal plane while sitting dynamically. The spine needs to change actively, "gathering" itself at each end of the stroke and elongating itself during each phase of the rowing action.

Because the rowing action is repeated continually, it makes sense to perform it as well as possible, to avoid injury, accrue all the health benefits, and simply to enjoy rowing for rowing's sake.

Applying the Alexander Technique to your rowing – as described in the earlier account of the Canadian sculler – can make a world of difference.

It can help you to identify what interferes with good technique; and how you can transform your experience of rowing *from the inside out.*

Largely unconscious habits of movement influence everything you do, not least your rowing.

A sedentary lifestyle has become the norm, through school, work and leisure. It impairs the ability to sit more actively, and to achieve the body swing needed in rowing for the transition from the drive phase into recovery.

So, the first question to ask yourself when seated, is: *am I sat or, can I sit?* That is, is my sitting *active* or *passive*?

Exploration 1: active v passive sitting

Video # 3, # 4, # 5 View at: www.youtube.com/rowingfromtheinsideout

- Sit towards the front of a flat, firm chair.
  - Put each hand, palm up, underneath your buttocks.
  - Feel the two knobbly protrusions at the base of your pelvis: these are your "sitting bones" (ischial tuberosities).
- Draw each one, in turn, a little way back, removing your hand; then adjust your weight over both sitting bones.
  - This should bring you over the centre of them, or even slightly forward.
- Next, *choose* to slump.
  - Can you feel how your weight shifts towards the *back* of the sitting bones and towards the tail bone?
  - This postural collapse loads the back, compresses the hip joints and makes it near-impossible to swing forwards from the hips at the release.
- Ease up once more over the centre of your sitting bones.
  - Play with leaning a little forwards and backwards over your sitting bones to help you become more aware of their role as "rockers", for they provide the foundation for the body swing in rowing.

When you are working at a desk, is it possible, then, to *sit*, and not to *be sat*? Or is your attention so focussed on the screen that you don't notice what your body is doing?

Evidence is mounting that *being sat* for most of the day is harmful for health and well-being. Rome wasn't built in a day, so aim to gradually build up the length of time you can *sit actively* at work.

Sitting *perched* on the front of the chair, without the need for support against your back, will allow your body to function better in due course. From the front of the seat, it's easier to get onto your feet, so less time may be spent in a state of immobility. Even better, use a *sitting-to-standing desk*, so that you can frequently change position during a work session.

More *active sitting* in the day will help you in your rowing action. The improved muscle tone and core stability that develops while rowing well will, in turn, assist your sitting at work. A *win-win* combination!

Exploration 2: from stand to sit; and sit to stand

Video # 6 View at: www.youtube.com/rowingfromtheinsideout

From stand to sit:

- Stand close to the front of a chair, with the backs of your legs touching.
  - Wrap the fingers of one hand loosely around the back of your neck, to feel any changes in your neck muscles as you move.
- As you sit down – just before the moment of arrival in the chair:
  - Did you feel any shortening and tightening in those muscles?
  - Did your head retract or pull backwards in relation to your neck?
- And, when you get up from the chair – at the moment of "lift-off" – does a similar tightening occur?
  - Do the shoulders tighten too?
  - Can you sense anything in your lower back?
- If you are not sure, put the chair to one side and try going all the way down to a squat, and back up again.
  - Do your heels stay down?
  - This more challenging movement will highlight any interference of the head-neck-back relationship.

Why is it so important to avoid "jamming" the neck?

Jamming indicates a problem in coordination, which has a knock-on effect throughout the body. If the neck is tightening, there's likely to be unnecessary tension in other places, especially in the shoulders and lower back.

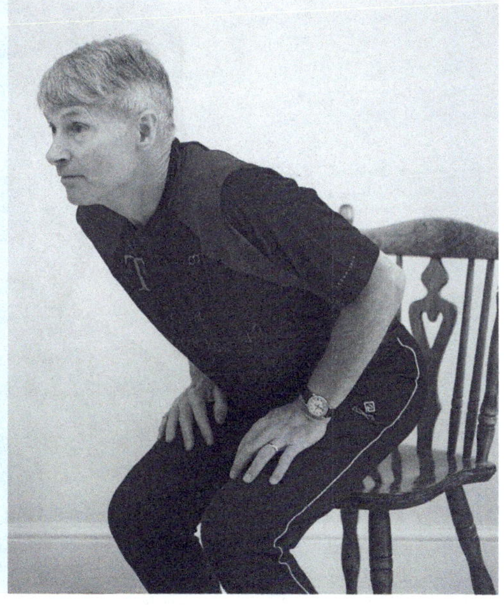

The head weighs a significant amount, about 9-12lbs (4-5Kg) in most adults. Pulling the head backwards and downwards at the beginning of the drive compresses the whole spine, making the lower back more vulnerable to injury. This stress in the neck puts work into the upper body which should be undertaken by the legs in rowing; and the drive will be weaker.

So, how to prevent the neck from tightening?

Try moving more slowly in the following explorations and attend to your neck as you come to sitting or standing. With patience, you may start to notice what is actually going on inside, and that awareness will start to alter what you do.

Before sitting or standing, send a thought to your neck to soften or release.

From sit to stand:

- Return to perching on the front of the chair, poised over the middle of your sitting bones.

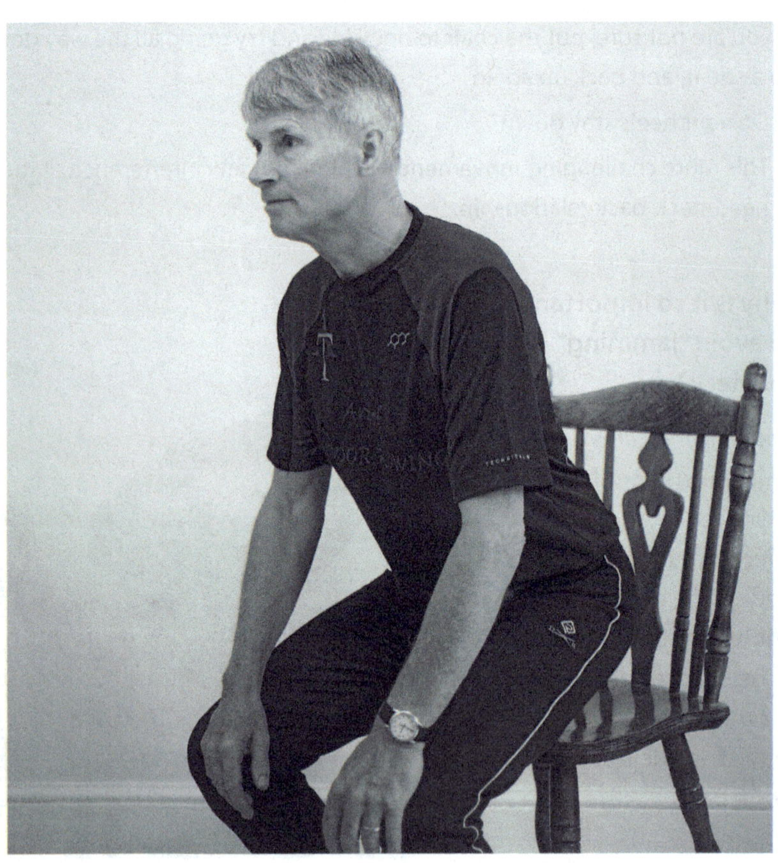

- Place both feet shoulders' width apart and flat, as close to the chair as possible, without the heels being lifted more than a millimetre or two off the floor. It's important that the heels can go down as weight transfers to the feet.
- Play with pivoting slowly forward and back over your sitting bone "rockers".
- Think of easing up along the spine and freeing the neck.
- As you slowly rock forward, notice the pressure building on the *balls* of your feet.
- That is the point at which most people launch themselves out of the chair, so try doing that to see how that feels.
- Ask yourself if the movement is smooth, or a little jerky?

▶ *Next* time you rock forward:

- *Refuse* to come to standing as weight shifts onto the balls of your feet.
- Pause: and then ease back to the vertical.
- Repeat a few times. This will begin to re-set your automatic response to your idea of getting up from a chair.

Now discover what happens as you lean forward, *wait for the heels to go down*, insted of pushing off the balls of the feet.

▶ Notice if "lift-off" occurs smoothly and easily, as the arches of the feet load fully and spring you to standing.

Exploration 3: locating the head-neck joint

Video # 7, # 8 View at: www.youtube.com/rowingfromtheinsideout

When asked where it is, people often mistake the "head-neck joint" – the *atlanto-occipital* joint – to be either at the *base of the back of the skull* (the nape of the neck), or at the *base of the neck*.

To help release tension in the neck, it's necessary to identify this joint's precise location. Either sitting or standing:

▶ Wrap one hand loosely again around the back of your neck.

- Nod your head gently and slowly from the *top* of the spine.
- Can you feel some movement in your neck as you nod *ever so gently*, or can your head move independently of your neck?

- To map the head-neck joint accurately:
  - Bring your fingers to the sides of your neck, at its base, and feel – through the muscle – the sides of your neck vertebrae (the transverse processes).
  - Walking your fingers up along the line of the bones, follow the gentle cervical curve forwards and then upwards, arriving just behind the ear lobes onto what are the mastoid processes of the skull.
  - Now, imagine a line between each of these two points.
  - Right in the centre is where the head-neck joint is located.
- Move your fingers around to the base of your skull, at the back, and try to nod your head from there.
  - It's likely you'll move the upper part of your neck *with* your head, and that the movement will be a little stiff.
  - Next, move your fingers down to the base of the neck, just above where you may feel the beginning of a "hump".

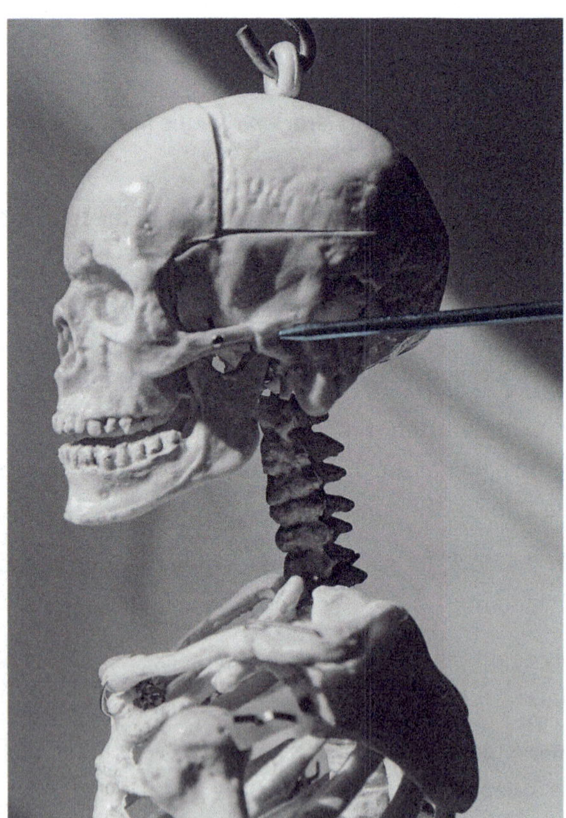

Pinpoint the height – on top of the spine – and central position of the head-neck joint, between the mastoid processes of the skull, directly behind the ear lobes.

  - Try to move your head from there. Notice if this feels more stressful, as the rest of the neck becomes involved in the movement.

- Finally, place your middle fingers onto the skull, just behind your ear lobes, with your forefingers just below, against the sideways-projecting *transverse processes* of the first cervical vertebra.
  - Invite your neck to release, and allow the head to slowly nod forwards from its rightful place on top of the spine – higher up and further forward than you might have thought it was.

  - Can you feel the difference? Your middle fingers should move a little with the skull – but your forefingers should remain still.
  - Go back to nodding from the back of the head, or from lower down the neck. The contrast should now be very clear.

Is it possible to carry this awareness – of the relationship between neck and head – into your rowing at each end of the slide, at connection and release?

- Finally, can you glance upwards a little, allowing the head to roll gently on top of the spine? Once more your middle fingers with be moved while the forefingers stay still.

If your neck is free of tension, your spine can elongate itself, during both the drive and recovery. The whole stroke will be more fluid, and your body will be much more comfortable.

Tuning in to where the head-neck joint actually is, is a necessary condition for discovering more freedom of your head on top of the spine.

Is there anything else you can do, to allow the head to move independently of the spine?

Try this further exploration:

Video # 9 View at: www.youtube.com/rowingfromtheinsideout

- Make a fist, with fingers clenched.
  - Imagine that your knuckles, pointing upwards, represent the crown of your head; the heel of the hand the chin, and the back of the hand the back of the head, with the wrist representing the neck.

- Now, soften and release your fingers, so that your fist begins to unclench.
    - Notice how your (imaginary) head begins to to release in a forward and upward direction.
    - And how the neck begins to release backwards and upwards.

The fist-clenching exercise shows the sort of "Doing" we get habituated to, even more so when we exercise.

The release is an "un-doing", facilitated by the power of the mind. We are embodied beings!

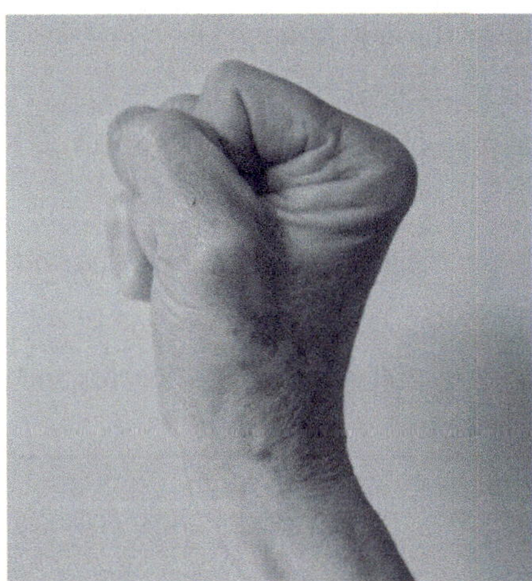

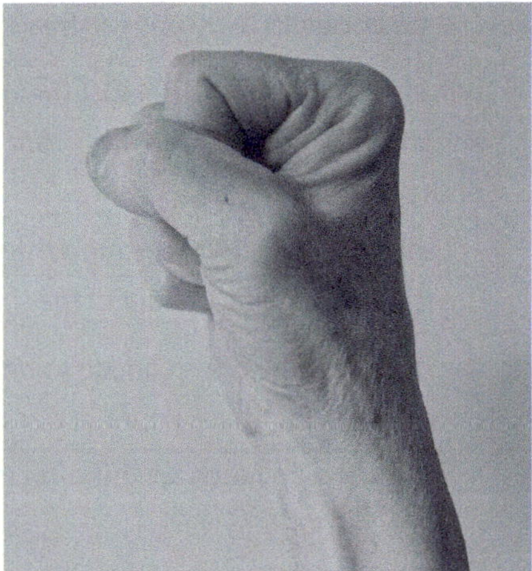

Exploration 4: Range of motion at the head-neck joint

Video # 10 View at: www.youtube.com/rowingfromtheinsideout

It is helpful in most contexts – and especially in rowing – to understand that the neck is *part of* the spine, and that its movement possibilities should not be forced, in relation to the rest of the spine.

First of all, make use of the range of flexion and extension available at the head-neck joint, which is approximately 15° in both directions. At each end of the slide, you can therefore avoid much unnecessary compression of the spine.

- At catch, rowers often stiffen the neck, and pull the head back and down.
- At the end of the drive, they commonly pull the head and neck forward and down.

How might this be avoided?

- Perch once more at the front of the seat.
    - Place one foot – with its heel remaining on the floor – a little in front of the other, which is underneath you, resting on the ball of the foot.
    - Wrap a hand loosely again, around the back of your neck.
    - Invite your neck to release, and your head to go *forward and up*.
    - Then, leaning forward a little – as if coming into connection/catch – allow your head to lead the movement in an "up and over" arc.
    - For this exercise, from gazing straight ahead at the start, let your eyeline drop about 15° or so, as the head moves through its arc.
- Without stiffening the back of the neck, notice if you can gaze straight ahead once more, by allowing your head to gently roll back a little, on top of the spine.
    - Think of *lengthening* through the *front of the neck*, as well as *releasing and widening* across the *front of the shoulders*.
- Next – and with care – choose to *deliberately* pull your head backwards and downwards, jamming your neck as rowers often do at catch.
    - See if you can feel how this affects you.

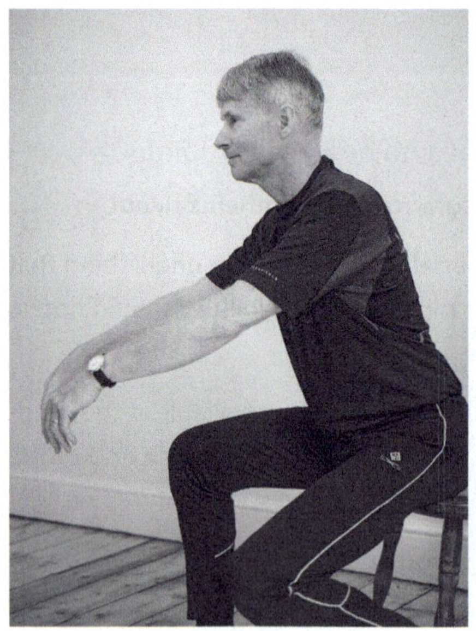

The catch with ease

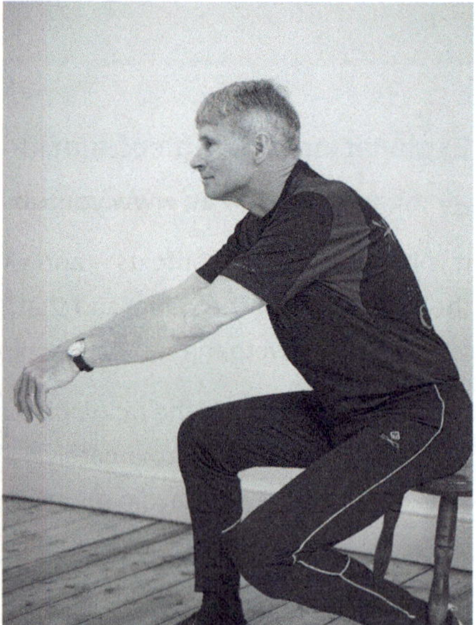

Upper body tensing

Now, to explore what happens to the head-neck balance at the end of the drive:

- Still perching at the front of the chair:
  - This time, wrap one hand around the *front* of your neck, underneath your chin.
  - Leaning slowly towards the back of the chair, activate your deep abdominal muscles to support the lower back, and gaze roughly 15° upwards.
- Next, allow the head to roll forwards, so that you are now looking straight ahead.
  - Contrast this with tightening your neck and pulling the weight of the head forward and down.
- To return to sitting vertically again:
  - Pull in the belly button more strongly and hollow the chest to spring upwards and forwards out of the pelvis.

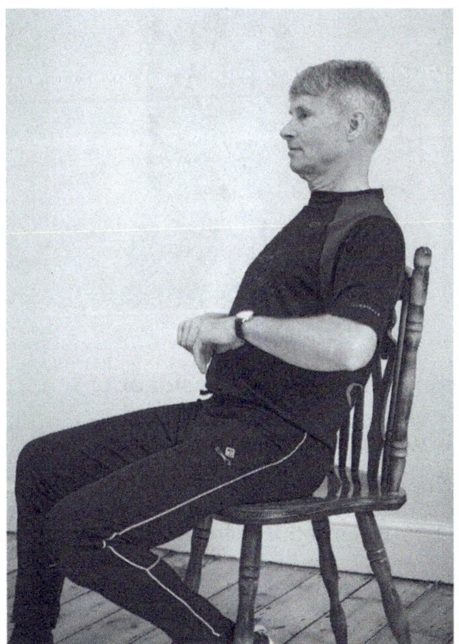

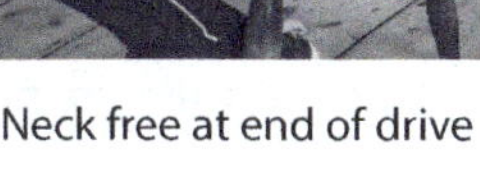

Neck free at end of drive

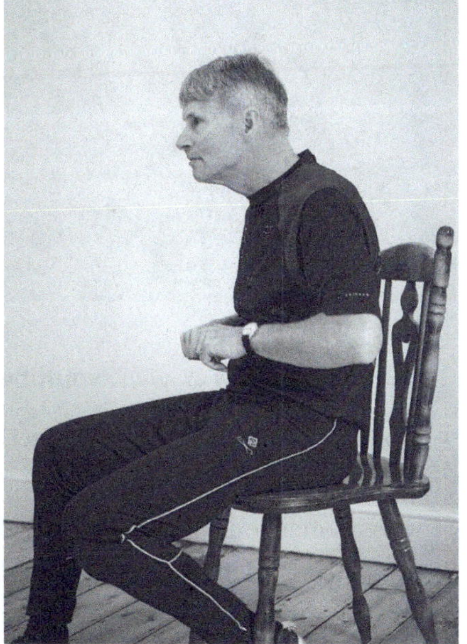

Neck and head pulling down

- Finally, see if you can rock slowly forwards or lean back – while gazing horizontally – and without stressing your neck.

Exploration 5: mapping the hip joints

Video # 11 View at: www.youtube.com/rowingfromtheinsideout

When the hip joints are mis-mapped, bending usually takes place in the lower back. Rowers especially would benefit from being crystal-clear about their location.

A common misconception is that the hip joints are located behind the hip *bones* – the *superior iliac spines* – which are prominent at the front of the pelvis. But this is way too high.

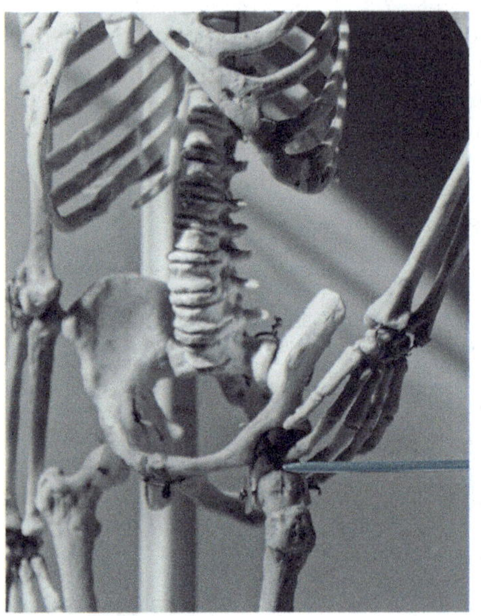

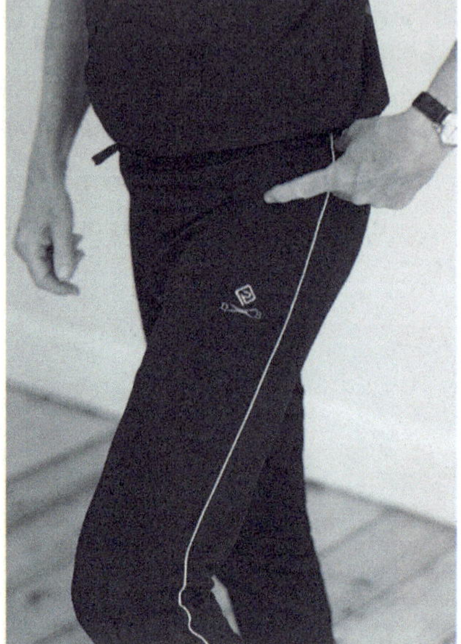

Video # 12 View at: www.youtube.com/rowingfromtheinsideout

- Come to standing, to identify precisely where the ball of the thigh bone (*femur*) articulates with the socket in the pelvis.
  - Feel where one hip bone is and slide your hand down from the hip bone to the top of the thigh.
  - Raise the knee on that side a little, to confirm (feeling through the muscle) that the hip joint is located significantly *lower* than the hip bone.
- Now trace the joint around to the side, as you lift the leg sideways (*abduction*), and all the way round to the back, to just in front of the sitting bone – the "rocker" – at the base of the pelvis.

- The leg can be moved independently in the hip joint without disturbing the lower back.
- Also note that the torso, including the pelvis, can be moved in relation to the legs.
- Both actions are needed in rowing.

Exploration 6: allowing more space in the hip joints

Video # 13 View at: www.youtube.com/rowingfromtheinsideout

Stand in your normal way. Can you feel any pressure on the hips and lower back?

Most people are quite unaware of whether this is the case, and it can take some time before pain or discomfort in these joints alerts them to the problem.

In exploring standing, the first question to ask is, *where is weight distributed on the feet?*

Play with these options:

- Shift your weight directly over the heels.
  - Do you feel your knees lock as the quads (the big muscles at the front of the upper thigh) tighten, and your lower back braces?
- Then shift very slightly forward so your weight is just in front of the heels – actually, directly over the ankle joints.
  - Can you feel your knees softening (but not bending) and the quads releasing?
- Next, shift weight further towards the balls of the feet.
  - Did you notice any signal of stress in the ankles, in maintaining balance?
  - Do your calves tighten and your back start to sway, possibly with the knees starting to bend as well?
  - Notice how the pelvis pushes forwards: does it feel as though you are sitting in a bucket? Hip mobility is reduced, and the lower back compressed.
- Finally, make the backwards and forwards movements over your ankle joints smaller and finer.
  - See if you can locate that "still point", where your weight is directly over the ankle joints. These are a little in front of – as well as above – the heels.

- An easy standing balance involves the weight *towards* – but *not directly over* – the heels.
- If the spine is now supported properly by the feet, legs and pelvis, *thinking* of releasing the neck muscles will be easier.

Video # 14 View at: www.youtube.com/rowingfromtheinsideout

The attitude of the pelvis.

In a sway back posture, the pelvis is thrust forwards and tilted backwards. In contrast, when you are well-balanced – and the navel is drawn-in subtly – your pelvis is drawn *further back* under the shoulders and *tipped forwards slightly*; this anterior tilt is more pronounced in the female pelvis.

- To feel the minimal work your lower, deep abdominal muscles need to do to contribute to an easy standing balance:

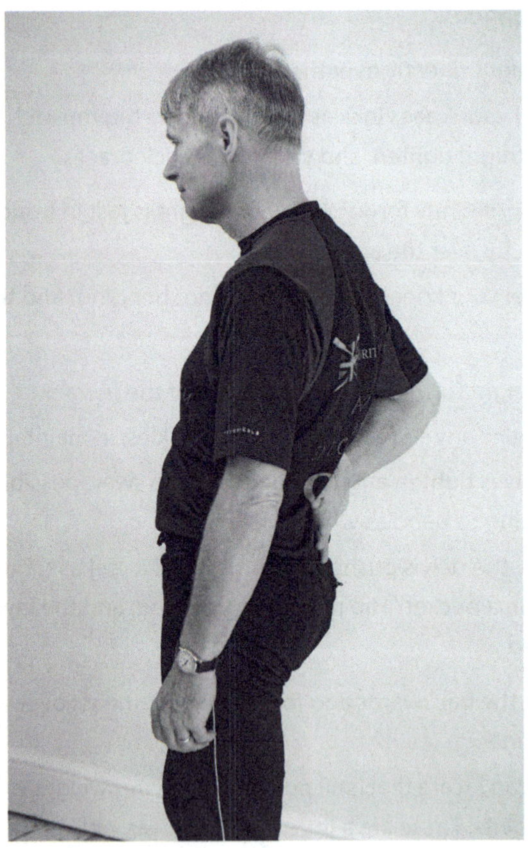

A typical sway back posture

- Place your hands over your lower abdomen – just above your pelvis – thumbs over the navel. Pull in the navel subtly to engage the deep abdominal muscles.
- This brings your back *back*, with the lower back *expanding* a little, instead of being "small".
- Your "behind" will be *behind* you. As long as your tail bone (*coccyx*) is dropping towards your heels, your buttocks will not be sticking out – even though you may feel that they are.
- Check in a mirror to see if your subjective sense matches what you can objectively see.

▶ Your tail bone will start to lift if it moves too far back, and you will indeed be arching your lower back, and sticking your bottom out.

Be sure to identify this in order to avoid it!

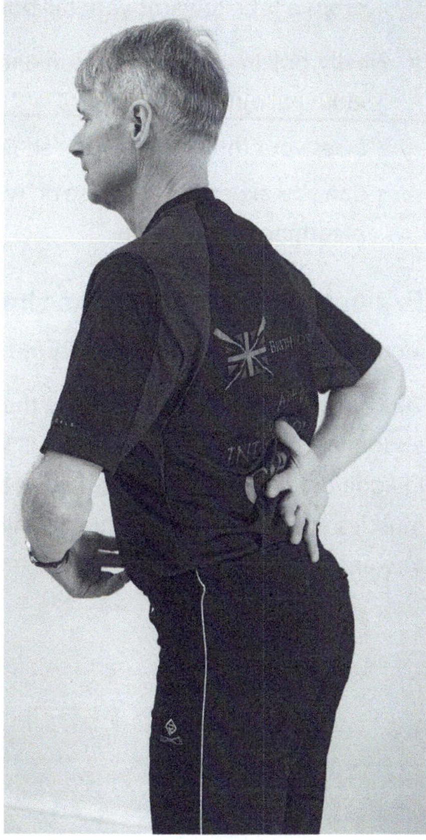

The role of your core muscles

- To feel the minimal work your lower, deep abdominal muscles need to do to contribute to an easy standing balance:
  - Once more place your hands over your lower abdomen – just above the pelvis – thumbs over the navel.
  - *Choose to collapse*: adopt a sway back posture and observe the deep abdominal muscles – those underneath your belly button – slackening off.
- Now draw in your belly button by millimetres towards your backbone.
  - Your deep abdominal muscles will tone-up, engage, activate – *not tighten*.
- Next, place the back of one hand against your lower back, with your little finger over the tail bone, and your thumb into the small of your back.
  - Sway back again.
  - Can you feel your lower back shortening and narrowing: your thumb ***drops*** a little towards your tail bone and your ribs draw closer together?
- Finally, pull in your belly button once more to activate those deep abdominal muscles.
  - Does your thumb rise a little again, as your lower back lengthens?
  - Can you experience a sense of "widening"? As a consequence, your breathing may deepen.

Exploration 7: hinging from the hips

Many rowers move into the recovery by reaching from the lower back.

This is more likely to happen when the rower leans back too far, and their deep abdominal muscles slacken. They will sink down into their hips and lower back. In addition, if the knees are locked at the end of the drive, the hamstrings (the muscles at the back of the thighs) will tighten. The rower will inevitably bend forwards from the waist.

Video # 15 **View at: www.youtube.com/rowingfromtheinsideout**

Kneeling

- Kneel tall, with the spine lengthened, your deep abdominal muscles switched on, and your pelvis tipped slightly forwards.
  - Place the back of one hand against your lower back, with your little finger resting on your tail bone, and the fingers of your other hand pointing to the hip joint.
- *Choose to slump,* and the pelvis will become more level.
  - Try to bend forwards. Can you feel the bending is mostly in your back, with only a little hinging taking place from the hips?

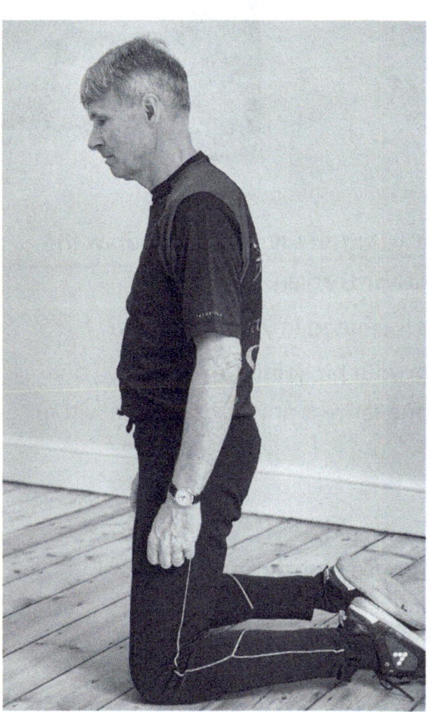

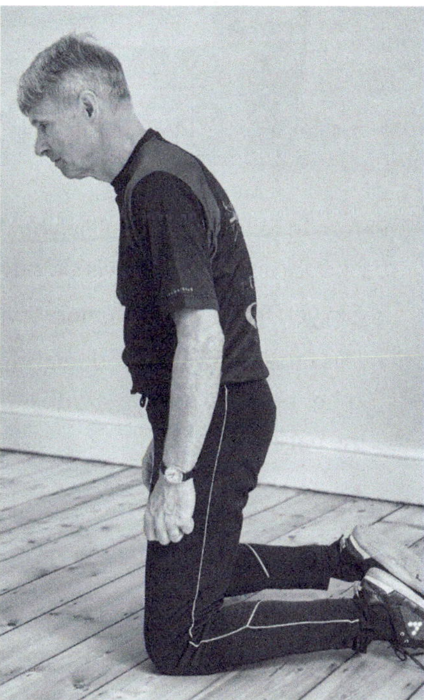

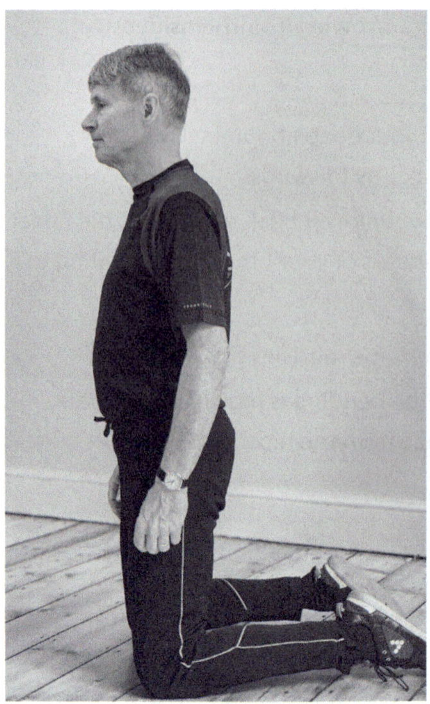

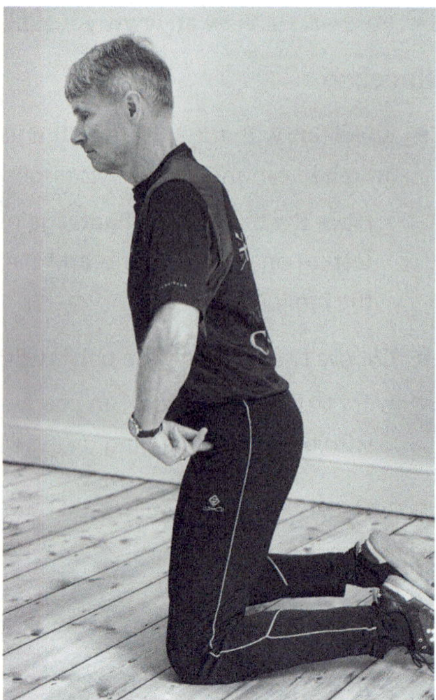

- Return to tall kneeling: pull in your belly button a little more to draw the back *back* and tip the pelvis slightly forwards again.
  - Can you feel how much more space is created in your hip joints?
  - This time can you pivot directly from your hip joints, followed by your knees bending *passively*, with little movement now taking place within the back?

Standing

Video # 16 View at: www.youtube.com/rowingfromtheinsideout

- With the back of one hand placed against your lower back as before – again to monitor any changes there – deliberately slump into a sway back posture.
  - Try to pivot forward a little from your hips.
  - Even knowing now exactly where your hip joints are located, you will probably notice that most of the bending takes place in your lower back.

- Return to standing in a more poised way, as described in *exploration 6*.
  - To hinge a little from the hips, pull in the belly button a little more strongly.
  - Feel your lower back moving back *as a whole* from your pelvis, which also moves back and tilts further forward, tipping your aligned spine forward.

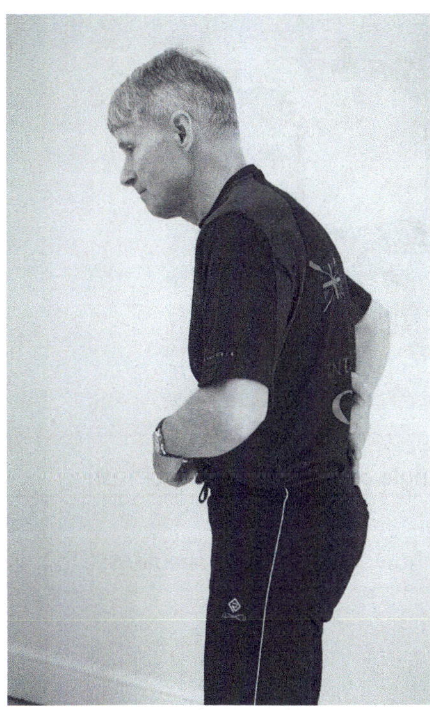

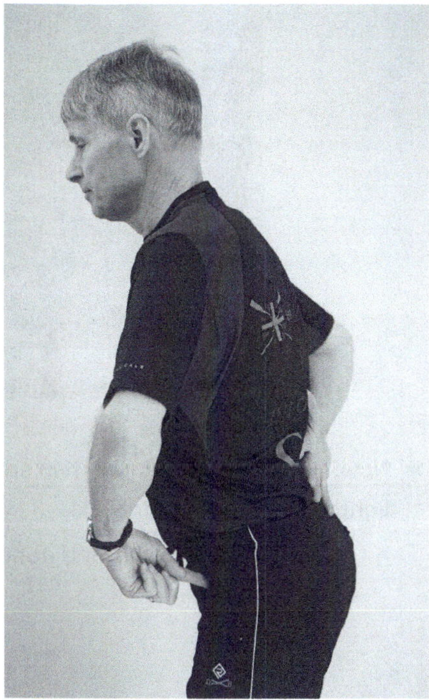

Exploration 8: pelvic rock and body swing

Video # 17 View at: www.youtube.com/rowingfromtheinsideout

- Bring a chair close to the edge of a door that is wedged wide open.
  - Perch on the front edge of the chair, over your sitting bones.
  - Move the chair even closer to the door, so that you are almost straddling its edge.
  - Hold the door handles lightly, with hooked fingers, and your arms bent approximately at right angles.

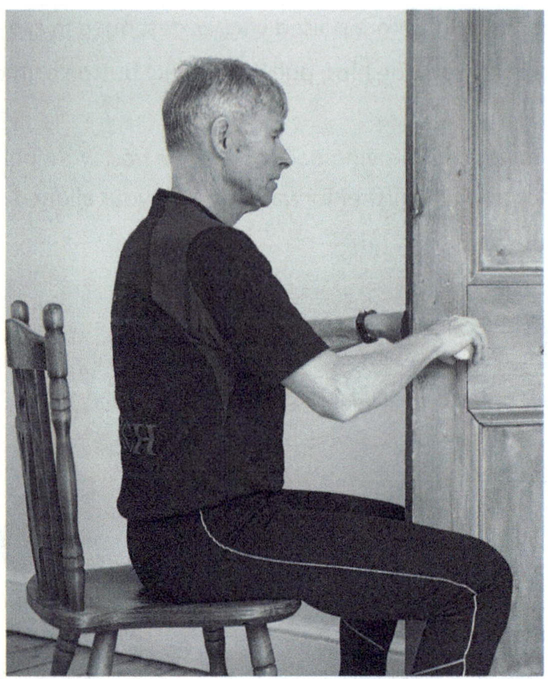

- Now, lean back by no more than an angle of 30°, with your back resting lightly against the chair back.
    - Choose to slump down, and notice how sluggish the movement is, to return to vertical.

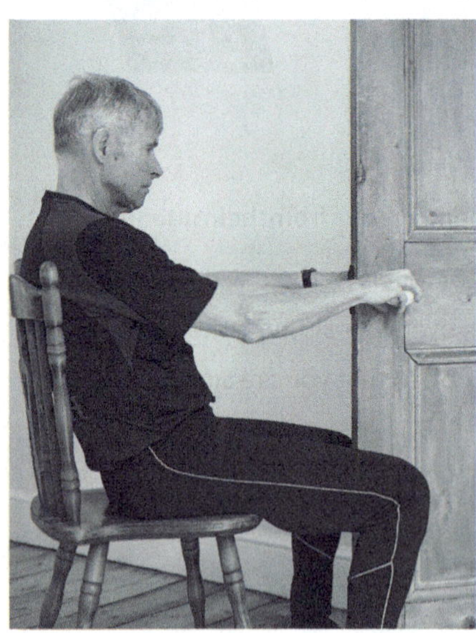

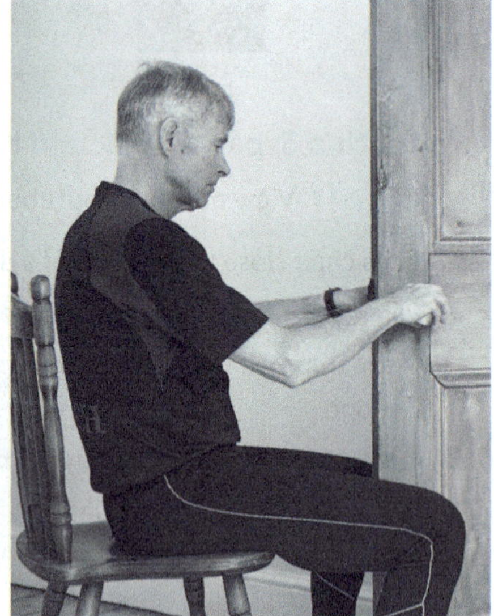

- This time, switch on your deep abdominal muscles more strongly as you lean back to then swing forwards.
  - Notice how your chest naturally hollows, as you lean back.
  - The lower back is held firm, stabilising it to prevent undue pressure and to limit the amount of lean back.
  - The pelvis rocks forward to support the forward body swing.
  - Notice if this makes your "return journey" easier.

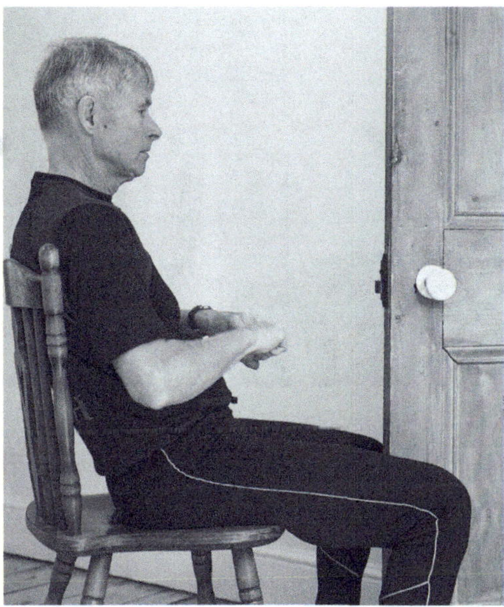

Stabilising the lower back on the swing backwards by engaging the deep abdominal musles and hollowing the chest.

- Next, having leaned back again, let go of the handles and straighten (*extend*) your arms *before* swinging your body forward.
  - In most rowing instruction, the sequence for the recovery is "arms away", and then "body swing". How does that feel?
- By way of contrast, try adding a subtle pull on the handles. This will help to initiate the countermotion of the forward swing.
  - To achieve this, just before the limit of "layback" is reached, pull lightly and quickly on the handles.
  - Backward motion is reversed as the body begins its swing forward – like an inverted pendulum – releasing the whole body up and over from the hips.
  - At the same time, let go of the handles and extend the arms.

So, the body can send the arms away, rather than the body follows the arms.

- Play with the timing.
  - Discover how the change of direction – from back swing to forward swing – is much quicker and easier than when the body's motion is reversed by that little pull on the handles, and the arms are "flung away".

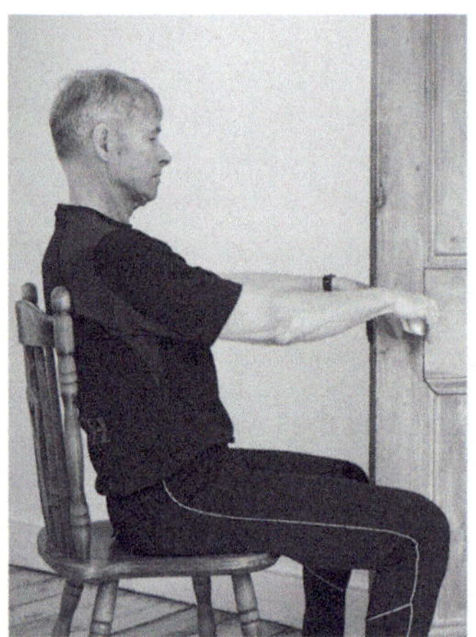
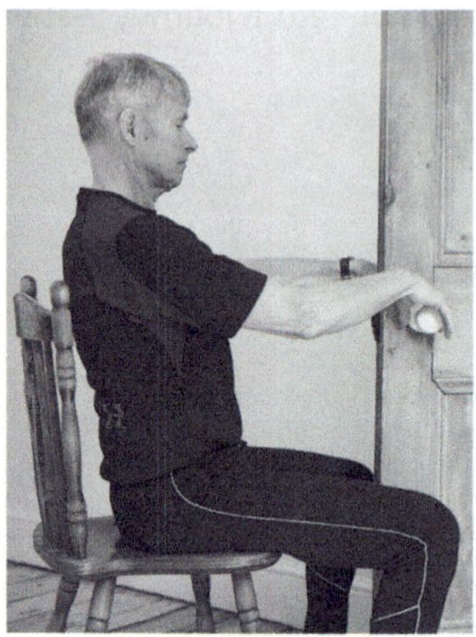

Beware of "chinning it": avoid pulling neck and head forward and downwards in advance of the rest of the spine. To help prevent this from happening, identify and exaggerate it:

- Lean against the back of the chair, slumped.
  - *Send* your hands away, and then initiate the forward movement of the body from the neck and head.
  - Can you feel how this compresses the spine even more?

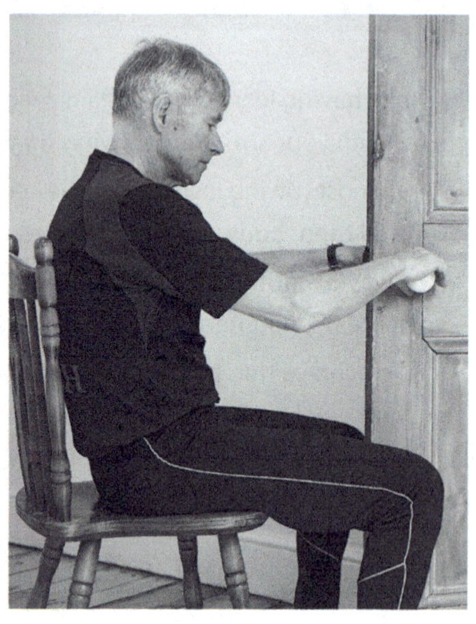

This is how the classic C-shaped spine of many rowers is created at the release, persists throughout much of the rowing stroke, and is compounded at the catch.

Exploration 9: the role of the "lats"

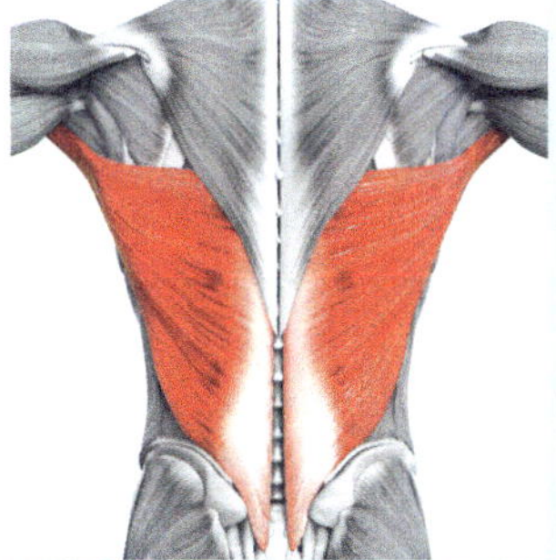

The *latissimi dorsi* are the broad back muscles, commonly known as "lats".

The lats attach the upper arms to the mid-thoracic spine, all the way down to the sacrum and to the lower tip of the shoulder blade. They are the largest muscles in the body, after the glutes.

The range of motion of the shoulders from protraction (reaching forward) to retraction (drawing back) – despite only a few inches – adds significantly to the length of the stroke.

Work the lats by drawing in the arms, in the pulling part of the stroke, taking strain off the weaker wrists and forearms.

Explore these small movements at home, or in the gym where you could use low weights on the resistance machines. Let the neck remain free of tension as you perform them:

Lat pull-down:

- Raise – but do not unduly tighten or "shrug" – the shoulders.
    - Then draw the shoulder blades down and closer together – your arms remaining straight – before allowing your elbows to bend.

Seated row:

- Reach forwards, maintaining length in the spine.
  - Avoid lifting the shoulders.
  - Draw your shoulders back, reeling in the arms by just a few inches – without bending them.
  - Then allow your arms to bend, to complete the arm draw.

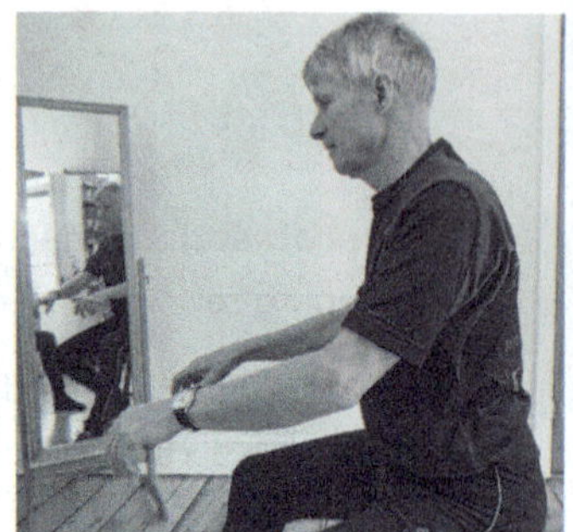

Exploration 10: hanging off the handles

Video # 18 View at: www.youtube.com/rowingfromtheinsideout

- Stand with your weight towards your heels, facing the edge of a door as before – but with the chair placed a little further away – and with the backs of your legs touching the chair.
  - Invite your shoulders to release and spread sideways, and then hook your fingers lightly around the door handles with your arms straight, but not tense.
  - Depending on the height of the handles, you may need to bend your legs a little, to take hold.
- Reminding your neck to release, allow your spine to lengthen itself and lean back from your ankles (not from your lower back), so that your weight is more directly over the heels.
  - Maintain the verticality of the spine as far as possible, hips still under shoulders.

- Trust the door handles to take your weight (if you were to let go of the handles, you would fall backwards).
- Check that the head has not pulled back and that you are not bracing yourself.

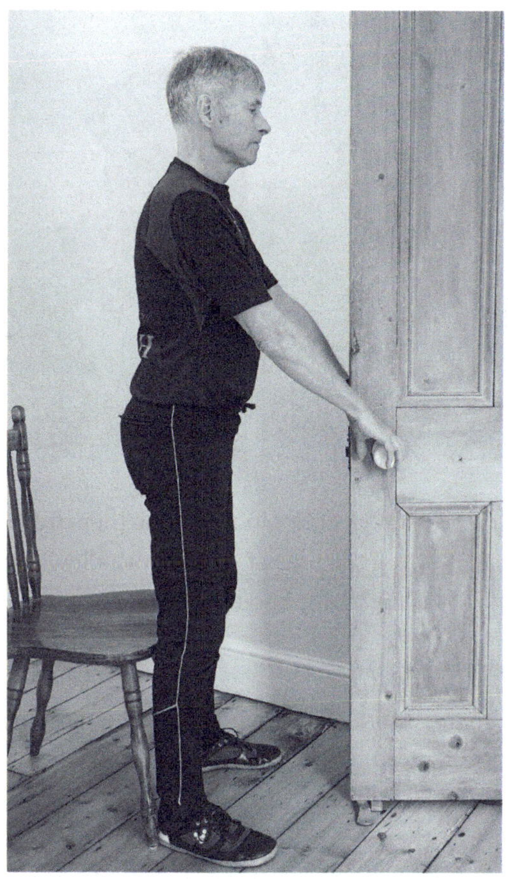

Simulate part of the recovery phase of the rowing stroke – by coming to sitting.

- Think of releasing up along your spine and allow your hips, knees, and ankles to bend.
  - The chair will interrupt your descent, and you should arrive sitting towards the *front* of the seat, with your back still close to the vertical.
  - It's possible that the heels may have lifted a little if your ankles are stiff. If so, move them a *small* distance forward, so that your heels could go down if weight is put onto the feet.

- Did you notice your fingers gripping? Release them from the handles and rest them, palms up, on the tops of your thighs, allowing the shoulder blades to draw *back and down* into the back.

Now to simulate catch/connection.

How to get up from the chair – by hanging your weight on the handles – is the main objective of this exploration. It's an insight into what should happen at *catch* and the beginning of the *drive*.

Begin by identifying what you should *prevent*:

- First, try getting out of the chair by pulling yourself forward, by bending your arms.
  - Can you feel your shoulders and neck tightening?
- Alternatively, *shove* with your legs.
  - Can you feel your lower back arching?

You can get up in both of these ways, but they are stressful.

Is it possible to rise from the chair with much less effort and without stiffening the body? Harnessing the power of your thinking, the "lift-off" may well surprise you: it just does itself when the right conditions are present. No "muscling" it.

Every part of your body is connected but, paradoxically, every part is in a dynamic opposition to its adjacent part.

- Once more, *release and widen* across the shoulders, to hold the handles lightly.
  - Invite your neck to release, to allow the head to orientate itself *forwards and upwards*, and your back to *lengthen and widen*.

In AT, this is what is meant by "giving directions".

These "directions" aim to prevent you from "Doing" it, and instead allow a release into movement, avoiding undue muscular effort.

- So, first, have the "up" direction in mind.
- Next, add in the direction: *back "back", away from the door.*
  - Think of this as though you are trying to pull the door handles towards *you*, rather than pulling *yourself* towards the door.
- Finally, without forgetting the "up" and the "widening" and the *back "back"*, allow the "down":
  - Simply *let the heels press* into the floor – and lift-off may occur, magically, smoothly and with minimal work.

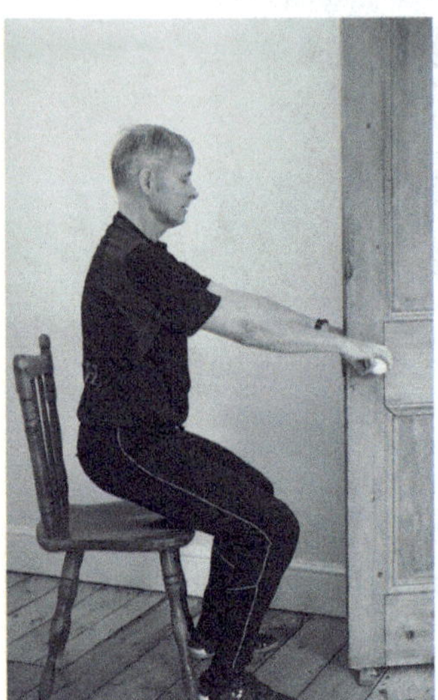  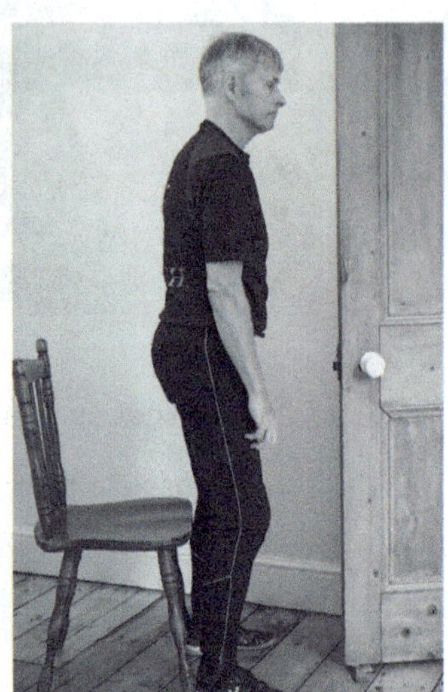

If this does not work immediately, experiment with deliberately "putting a spanner in the works" – that is, *exaggerate what needs to be avoided* – and then let it go.

For example:

- Stiffen your neck and pull the head *back* (as many rowers do at catch); then let go of that tension.
- Clamp your shoulders *upwards and inwards*; then *release them sideways, backwards and downwards.*
- Empty your lungs of air, relax, and hang your weight heavily on the door: you will stay chair bound.

Once you have this exercise working, increase the challenge by replacing the chair with a lower stool, and eventually arrive in a full squat. Because the door handles will be relatively higher, take extra care not to tense the shoulders. With your weight over your heels, pressure on your knee joints will be reduced.

Discover by this error-correction that it is necessary to have both the "up" and the "down", the "left" and the "right", and the "forward and back" of the relevant parts.

In the end everything must connect – yet be in opposition to everything else. If you neglect even one part, it simply cannot work.

Help increase the ankle flexibility needed at connection/catch by squatting in this way, supported by hanging off door handles.

This exploration rehearses what rowers call "suspending your weight on the handles".

Video # 19 View at: www.youtube.com/rowingfromtheinsideout

Now you have more awareness – and some thinking tools to draw on – the next chapter will look at how best to warm up before rowing.

5

Warming up

Here's a question: Should I go straight into a rowing workout, or should I prepare for it? And if so, what's the best way to do that?

- Even if you don't have much time, remind yourself that there is no rush.
- If you're feeling really stressed – tension in your neck, back and shoulders will be the main indicators – lie down in the "AT releasing position" for a few minutes.
  - See below for a full description of this.

Someone once said, "whenever I get the urge to exercise, I lie down until it passes off!". While that sounds like a lame excuse for not moving enough, the point is *what am I bringing to my exercising?*

The next consideration is, how much time should I spend preparing and warming up – and how much time is needed afterwards, for cooling down and stretching?

- The simple answer is to allow five minutes or so, before and after you row.
  - More, if you intend to row a longer, or more demanding, work-out.
  - *Après-row* will be addressed in chapter 9.

If you feel good to go, you could simply start by:

- Rowing at a low stroke rate – say, 16-18 strokes per minute at light pressure – and up to ¾ slide. Do so *mindfully*.
- Alternatively, row *parts* of the stroke, starting with the arms and shoulders, then pelvic rock and body swing, and on up to quarter-slide, half-slide and three-quarter slide, before reaching full slide.
  - See the next chapter for a full description of this.

Check in with yourself:

- *How am I today?* What's working, where is there any stiffness or tension?
  - Invite those places in the body to soften or release, and proceed with care until you experience more ease.
  - If that does not happen quite soon, you probably need to stop...and lie down.
  - Think about how to address the issues that have presented themselves.
  - It's okay to come back to rowing another day.

The AT releasing position

Lying down in what is called "semi-supine" or "constructive rest" in the Alexander world – or what I call "the AT releasing position" – has many benefits.

Quieten your mind, calm your breathing, release tension and discomfort, feel more whole, and cultivate an expanded posture.

- Set aside 5-10 minutes daily as a preventive strategy – and at other times as needed:
  - Find enough floor space to lie down on your back with your legs bent, feet flat, and where you are able to spread your arms.
  - A rug or exercise mat may make it more comfortable, but a mattress is way too soft.

- Place your feet shoulders' width apart, and a foot or two away from your body.
  - Let the knees roll in and out a little, and then settle, so that there is as much pressure on the inside as the outside of the feet; the legs are not fixed in position but held dynamically in balance.
- *Head support:* next to nothing under the head may be all that is required, or you may need several inches of support.
  - Place up to two or three soft back books under your head, with the thinnest one on top.
  - This makes it easy to remove the top book as tension in the neck and back diminishes, as you relax, and you need less support.

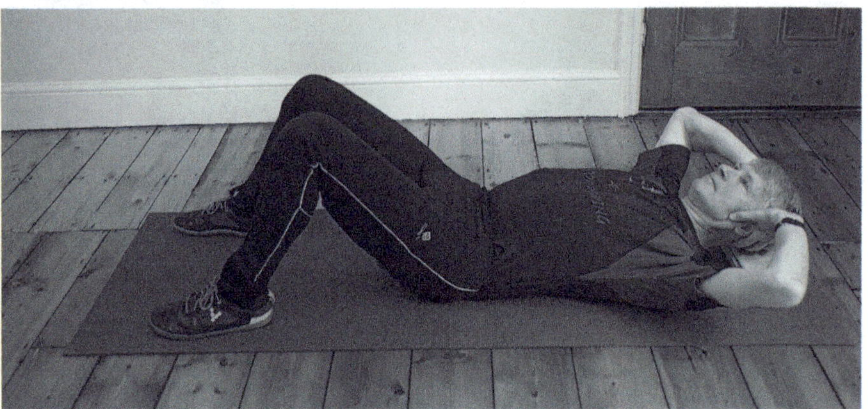

- With your hands, lift your head a little off the books, and then let it come to rest.
  - Avoid using your neck muscles. You might find that the weight of your head – 9-11lbs/4-5Kg – surprises you!
  - If the height of support is about right, you will be looking upwards and roughly 10-15° in the direction of your feet.
  - If the support is too high, the neck and head will be pushed forward on the rest of your spine.
  - With *too little* support, it will be harder to release tension in the back of the neck and lower back.
  - If in doubt, begin with a *little* more than you might think you may need; you can always lower the support after a while.

- If space is limited, rest your hands on your hips and lower abdomen – or on the lower ribs – with your elbows out.
- Another option is to let your arms extend out to the side, palms up; the fingers, slightly curled, will be off the floor. This will start to draw the shoulder blades deep into the back, helping to reverse the hunched posture from spending too much time looking at screens.
- If the shoulders remain comfortable, you could extend your arms a little further, in a wide V-shape, so that the hands reach beyond your head.
    - This will help you become more aware of both the length and breadth of your back.

Setting aside some time every day in this "releasing position" will help greatly in undoing postural tensions.

And if you can take the opportunity to work with an AT teacher, the following instructions will become clearer:

- On your own, you might want to dictate them onto a smartphone so as to talk yourself through them.
- Remember, the following "directions" are largely *preventive*, to stop you from clamping joints and tensing muscles – patterns which are especially likely to be triggered when there's any idea of "doing exercise".

- Note that the "forward" component of the "forward and up/out" direction (explained below) is already taken care of by the book support.
- Also note that this is nothing to do with stretching physically – however tempting that might be.
  - It's using the mind to *invite* what leads to the minutest separation of joint surfaces, as well as reducing tension in the associated soft tissues.
  - At first you will barely be able to feel this happening, on your own.

Try giving these directions – which are messages to the relevant parts of the body – in sequence:

Begin with what Alexander called the "Primary" directions.

- Let the neck release, to allow the head to ease out from the top of the spine...
- To allow the back to lengthen and widen.

Then add in these "Secondary" directions:

- Let the knees be directed up to the ceiling, up out of the hips and ankles.
- Let the shoulders release and spread sideways, upper arms away from the shoulder sockets, forearms out of the elbow joints, hands out of the wrists, and release all the many joints in the hands and fingers.

And then give all of those directions, together if you can!

To promote further release in the back:

- Draw up the knees – one at a time – toward your chest.
  - Renewing the directions, let the weight from the inside of *one* heel transfer to the *other*, so that, as the knee begins to fall inward, you can draw it toward the chest easily. It will follow an arc.
- Release the shoulder on the same side and hook your fingers – spread wide – around the inside of your shin bone, close to the knee.
  - Then hook the fingers of your *other* hand through those of the first hand, so that all the fingers lie *under* the palms, around the shin bone – rather than above, on the backs of the hands.

- If you grip the fingers together, you will tense the wrists and shoulders.
- Notice if your neck is still free of tension. Invite it to release again.

▶ While thinking of the spine lengthening, let the shoulders release and spread sideways, continuing the extension to the elbows to pull apart from each other and down, toward the feet.

- This will draw the knee closer to the chest, without elevating the shoulders or clamping them.
- In turn, this will release tension in the lower back on that side, as well as across the middle and upper back.
- Hold for up to half a minute, inviting more and more release without creating extra tension.

▶ Repeat on the other side.

This procedure will also help you to achieve the compression of the legs at catch/connection, while maintaining as much length and width in the torso as possible

To allow more space in the lower back after its release:

▶ You will need to adjust the position and attitude of the pelvis. Again, this is not to be a stretching but an *easing out* of the lower back.

- Leaving the neck alone, pull the belly button in to flatten the lower back, and use the legs to lift the pelvis an inch or two off the floor.
- With your hands at the sides of the pelvis, tilt it backward gently, so that the base of the spine is moved a little further away from the head. And then let it rest.

- Repeat this head and pelvis adjustment as required.
  - Note that the drawing of the knees to the chest only needs to be done once.

Before coming to standing:

- To mobilise the lower back:
  - Rock the knees a little to one side – engaging your core – and then back to centre.
  - Then rock to the other side.
  - Gradually increase the range of motion.
- To get up, release your neck, and let the eyes lead the head gently to the right, your body, and left arm, and leg, following.
  - From the side, roll over onto all fours.
  - Make fists, and bring them between the knees, tucking your toes under.
  - Supporting the weight of the body on the arms, rock backward until you can get the heels down, the hands coming off the floor.
  - Bring the body closer to the vertical from the hips, and then press the inside of the heels down, to straighten your legs.
  - Finally, relax the shoulders to look forward.

"Soft" stretching

Static stretches, held for up to half a minute, will restore or extend your range of motion. They are best performed *after* you have rowed, or in between sessions, so long as the body is not cold. See Chapter 9 for these.

"Soft", "dynamic" or "ballistic" stretches are a great way to warm up the body *before* rowing. Their main purpose is to lubricate joints and to ease the body into a moderate range of movement.

Indoor rowing or sculling should be a symmetrical activity. Many of the following movements – derived from Tai-chi preparatory exercises – involve rotation into asymmetry, to help bring the body back into symmetry. Note these points:

- Whatever the particular exercise you're doing, try to be aware of your whole body, and leave your neck free of tension.

- Relatively effortless movement can be generated by loading the arches of the feet.
- Any exercise requiring balancing on one leg can tone up core muscles.
- You may find that many of these exercises connect naturally to an easy breathing rhythm.
- Each time you repeat a movement, pay attention to the process, extending the range of motion gradually.
- As a rough guide, up to five repetitions of each movement should be sufficient. These exercises start from the top of the body and work downwards.

Video # 20 View at: www.youtube.com/rowingfromtheinsideout

Head, neck and upper spine rolling

Stand, as described in detail in the previous chapter, *User's Manual*, with your feet roughly shoulders' width apart, your weight *toward* the heels and knees soft, with your hands resting on your hips.

- Invite the neck to release, so the head is delicately balanced and free to move, at the *very* top of the spine.
  - Hollowing the chest, and pulling in the belly button more strongly, *glance down to the feet*, with your head, neck and upper spine flexing.
  - At the same time, feel the top of the thigh muscles and "glutes" (gluteal muscles) working, so that your hips remain under your shoulders.
  - Continuing the movement, *glance across to the left.*
- As the left arch loads, "borrow" some impetus from it to *glance up to the left, breathing in.*
  - Then roll the head, neck, and upper spine to *glance up to the right.*
  - Is your neck free enough for the head to roll itself?
- Without stopping, *glance down to the right, breathing out.*
  - Come back to the centre, following through to the left to repeat the circular motion.

- To reverse direction:
  - The next time you glance down to the *left, leave the breath out and roll back to the right, pressing the right arch into the floor to glance up to the right, breathing in.*
  - Then *circle up and across to the left*, and so on.

Shoulder rolling with spinal flexion and extension

- Actively hollow your chest and pull in the belly button strongly, to activate the lower, deep abdominal muscles.
  - At the same time, as before, "sit on your big muscles", so that your hips remain under your shoulders.
  - Feel the arches of your feet "spreading" on the floor.
  - Allow your shoulders to roll *forward*, the arms bending at the elbows, palms facing *sideways* and resting on the *fronts* of the thighs.
- Press the feet into the floor to lift the shoulders up, toward the ears.
  - Only then, *let the head rise to glance up,* without stiffening your neck.
  - *Turn your hands so the palms face upwards*, the little fingers in contact with the sides of the chest.
- Draw the shoulders *back and downwards*.
  - Allow your chest to soften, relax the shoulders and then repeat.

One arm windmilling

- Start with the *right foot a little in advance of the left*, with more weight shifted onto it – a comfortable lunge position.
  - Put the *right* arm "out of action" by resting the back of your hand comfortably on your lower back/pelvis.
  - Imagine a glass wall to your *left,* along which the *left* hand can lightly brush, in a circular motion.
- *Shift back*, letting the arm swing back.
  - The *left arch loads*.
  - "Borrow" energy from the arch of the foot to raise the arm, *breathing in*.
  - As the arm approaches the top of its arc, slow its movement down, looking to the fingernails and extending the fingers.

- *Shift forward*, releasing the shoulder, elbow, and wrist, so that as the arm drops in an arc, any acquired tension releases, and the palm now faces inward; breathe out.
  - Repeat.
- To *change direction*, once the arm has swung back, *leave the breath out* and *shift forward*, allowing the arm to swing with it.
  - *Load the right arch to lift the arm, turning to the left*, brushing the hand against that imaginary wall again, *breathing in*.
  - Again, *slow down toward the top of the movement*, extending the fingers, looking at the fingernails.
  - *Shifting your weight back*, relax the shoulder, dropping the elbow, and relaxing the wrist.
- Repeat the whole cycle on the other side.

Sculling arms, awakening the fingers (optional extra)

The sculling action of the arms draws the hands close together during each phase of the stroke and separates them toward the end of each phase.

It is a beautiful and satisfying motion and worth doing – even if it's only possible otherwise on the top-end rowing simulators, or in sculling.

And you can enliven the fingers, so that they are less like stiff claws gripping the handle of the rowing machine.

- Use the lunge again, while standing, or use a sitting lunge, with one foot forward and flat, and the other foot tucked under a little, its heel off the floor:
  - Shift your weight *forward*, directing your *fingers forward*, and the hands will naturally separate until they are wider than shoulders' width.
  - Enjoy the experience of *widening your back*, while maintaining as much length as possible.
  - *Put your mind into your front heel* to press it down, at the same time curling your fingers – starting with the little fingers – as though wrapping them lightly around oar handles.
  - With the whole body rocking *back*, your right hand draws back slightly, in advance of – and underneath – the left hand.

- And then, with the shoulders drawing your hands back, your elbows begin bending, and the hands separate toward the ribs at the sides of the chest wall.
- Next, release *up and out* of the hips and, without delay, shift *forward* again, with your right hand moving slightly in advance of the left and underneath it, flicking the fingers *down and away* – starting with the index fingers, through to the little fingers – extending the wrists a little as the hands separate once again.

▶ Swap your feet around to change position, and repeat.

Shifting weight and turning the waist, swinging the arms

▶ Place your feet a little wider than shoulders' width and turned slightly out.

- Bend your legs a little, with your weight *toward* the heels and staying upright, at the same time engaging your deep abdominal muscles, plus the tops of your thighs and glutes.
- Shift to the *left*, turning outwards to the *left*, while swinging your arms loosely with a large circular movement, so that they briefly "wrap" around your waist.
- Keep your knees pointing *forward,* so that the twisting motion takes place mostly in your spine and hips and does not stress the knees.
- Then shift *right* and turn *right,* swinging the arms to again wrap around the waist.

▶ To turn the opposite way:

- The next time your body arrives over the *left* leg, having turned out, keep your weight on *that* leg and turn *in* – to the *right* – again wrapping the arms around the waist.
- Then shift *right* while turning left. This variation creates a smaller circling movement of the arms than the first movement.

Circling the hips

▶ With your feet shoulders' width apart, and your hands resting on your hips:

- Roll your pelvis to the *right* and then swing *forward* and to the *left*, swinging *back* and to the *right*, completing an oval-shaped movement.
- The head should remain in the centre, though it tilts a little to balance the movement of the pelvis.

- To circle the other way, as your pelvis swings *forward* and to the *left*, pause:

Then circle to the *right* and *back* in a clockwise direction.

Imagine a little spherical object rolling smoothly around the inside of your abdomen, synchronising with the movement of the pelvis.

Balancing on one leg, rotate the other leg

The purpose of this movement is to further mobilise the hip joints.

- This time place your feet a little wider than shoulders' width apart, with your feet turned slightly *outwards*.
  - Bend your legs a little, with your weight toward the heels, staying upright.
  - Engage your deep abdominal muscles, the tops of your thighs, and glutes.
- Move your head across, so that it is aligned above the *right thigh*.
  - Keep looking *forward* while you turn your body to the *right*, putting your weight to the inside of your right heel.
  - Then *press the left heel*, through to the ball of the foot, "into" the floor.
  - From the right arch, raise your *left* knee and toes.
  - Circle out to the *left,* to open the hip joint.
  - Relax your leg and foot *down* to the floor again.
  - Gradually increase the range of movement.
- Repeat on the other side.

Balancing on one leg, swing the other leg forward and backward

With counter-balancing rotational movement through the torso, this exercise eases out the hamstrings and hip flexors.

- Stand with the feet in line with each other, a little apart.
  - Centre the head over the top of the *right thigh*, with your weight toward the inside of the heel.
  - Invite the neck to remain free of tension.
  - Swing the *right arm* back, and draw the *left leg* back as your *left arm* releases forward, to counterbalance the body.
  - Then "borrow" some energy from the *right arch,* to swing the *left leg forward and up.*

- And, while turning the body to the *left*, reach forward toward the *left* leg with the *right* arm, as the *left* arm swings back.

▶ Repeat on the other side.

Rolling the knees

▶ Bend your hips, knees and ankles, and rest your hands on your knees.

- Starting with the weight toward the heels, *roll forward* along the *outside edges* of the feet toward the little toes' side, with the *inner edges* of the feet lifting (inversion).
- Then *roll back,* from the big toes' side of the insteps to the heels, with the *outer edges* of the feet lifting (eversion).
- ***Make sure to roll the knees only in this direction***, to lubricate the knee joints and to avoid stressing them.

Squatting

▶ Stand with the feet hips' width apart, with your weight toward your heels.

- Raise the arms above the head, without arching your lower back.
- Then, releasing the shoulders and bending the elbows, press the hands *forward and downwards* – as though splashing in water – at the same time bending the hips and knees.
- Keep looking *forward,* without stiffening the neck.
- The hands continue to move *backward;* and then release the wrists and shoulders to "splash" the backs of the hands.
- This will re-load the arches of the feet again, so that you can again "borrow" from them to stand up and repeat the movement.

▶ Gradually ease lower, toward a squat, *keeping your heels on the floor.*

- Remember to bend the hips first, followed by the knee bending *passively;* make sure your weight stays toward the heels, and you will spare your knee joints.
- Finally, on returning to standing, rise onto the balls of the feet, extending the ankle joints.
- Let your weight come back toward the heels before bending again.

You're now primed for an enjoyable row. Part 3 will unravel the secrets of the rowing stroke.

PART 3

6

Moving up the slide

Because [drills] draw attention to a part of the stroke, rather than the whole, they have to be pursued judiciously. The perfect stroke is a perfect gesture: seamless, spontaneous, graceful.

Frank Cunningham, *The Sculler at Ease*

Have you ever seen anyone on a rowing machine at the gym, practise *parts* of the stroke? Out on the water, rowers do so as an essential part of every training session. They hone the main elements in the narrative of the stroke, to improve their ability to row well through the whole stroke.

The word "drills" – often used in this context – is probably best put to one side because of what that word can imply: mindless, mind-numbing, boring repetition of the same pattern of movement.

By way of contrast, is it possible to approach the key skills of rowing in the spirit of playfulness and exploration?

How to practise constructively

Ask yourself, "how can I rehearse each skill in the most effective way, and with the least amount of physical effort?"

Force of habit, as explained earlier, often feels right. That means that you may not be able to sense what you are doing – at first – and this blocks you from discovering what you actually need to do. If you simply repeat what *isn't* working, you keep digging yourself into the same hole. *Practice makes permanent*, whether good or bad.

Is it possible to pay more attention to those cues coming from the kinaesthetic ("movement sensation") sense? Tiny sensors in joints and muscles can accurately inform you of how the body is being coordinated, and the amount of muscular work being done. If you start by moving quite slowly, it may be easier to sense these cues.

The best way to *know* how you are performing is via objective feedback. Ideally an observer would be both an Alexander teacher and a perceptive rowing coach, but one or the other would be a good deal better than nothing.

The alternative is to become your own expert, in time, by refining your self-observation skills.

Follow FM Alexander's lead: set up a mirror or two at different angles or use your smartphone to film yourself. Compare what you *feel* you are doing with what you can *see* yourself doing.

To observe with clarity takes time, but comparing and contrasting these two sources of information will guide your progress. With practice, the gap between *what you think you are doing* and *what is really happening* will gradually diminish.

Preliminaries: avoid strapping yourself in

Having come to sitting on the rowing machine – *notice how you did that* – the first thing that nearly everyone does is to tighten the strap(s) around their feet. Apparently for safety, this is to avoid falling off the back of the machine at the end of the drive.

However, if you leave the straps loose, you might discover how to save yourself from poor technique: by affirming your connection to the foot stretcher *through the soles of your feet*, which is the key to good rowing. All will become clear shortly.

Experiment with the height of the foot stretcher: setting it lower makes it easier to achieve a forward lean from the hips; higher, makes it less challenging on stiff ankle joints. Find the best compromise.

Start by rowing lightly, at 18-20 strokes per minute (spm) for a couple of minutes, to warm up and tune in to how your body is reacting.

Enjoy the whole stroke – don't worry about doing it "correctly" – and notice if anything comes to your attention. For example:

- How loose is your hold on the handles?
- At catch, are your shoulders relaxed – but engaged? Is one shoulder higher than the other?
- How do your feet make contact with the foot stretcher during the rowing stroke?
- Is the recovery phase *unrushed* – approaching twice the length of the drive phase?
- Are you able to smile as you approach catch?
- During the drive, can you feel *all* parts of your body, in sequence, coming smoothly into play, as the movement of the handle accelerates and then follows through into the recovery without interruption?
- Are you breathing easily?
- What feels stiff, awkward, jerky, or uncomfortable?

There is much to begin to think about…so just make a note of what comes to your attention.

Although rowing is primarily a *pushing* exercise from the legs – rather than a *pulling* one with the arms – the arms need to be attended to first. They transmit the power, on the indoor rower, to the handle, and to the oars in sculling. As you work your way up the slide, the legs will progressively come more into play.

Start your exploration of the stroke by sitting on the rower towards the *back* of the slide, with your legs straight but knees soft, and leaning back *slightly*. The body should remain still and firm, the neck free of undue tension.

Beware of slumping

- Identify what a "relaxed" position feels like, and what it leads to.
  - *So, choose to slump*. Can you sense any pressure on your lower back and hip joints?
  - If yes, you're probably not engaging your deep abdominal muscles and your weight will be too far back on the sitting bones as your pelvis goes into an extreme backwards tilt. (You'll notice there is a cut-out at the back of the seat, where the tailbone would press, should you sway back way too far.)
  - As a consequence, you risk your back continuing to compress itself through the recovery; unchecked, this leads to the familiar C-shaped back of the rower.

    - And at catch, it's impossible to get your weight fully onto your feet to generate the most powerful stroke.

- Instead of slumping, now think "up" along your spine, and switch on your core muscles, pulling your belly button in towards the backbone.
    - Release up out of your hips and make sure you are not too far back over your sitting bones. This requires just the right amount of muscular work in the right places.
    - Let your feet remain flat on the foot stretcher.

How to hold the handle(s)

In rowing instruction, addressing the handle(s) is nearly always framed in terms of *gripping*.

If you look at close-up photos of scullers in action, you'll often see grim determination on their faces, the handles sometimes gripped too far in, and the thumbs pressing onto the handles as if to prevent water from escaping from the ends of hosepipes.

Perhaps more "grip" is needed on the language? Just how relaxed can *your hold* be?

The more attention you can pay to *inviting the release of tension*, the more *letting go* will reveal itself over time, rather like peeling layers off an onion.

Rowers who put time in on the water often struggle with blisters. All sorts of remedies are suggested to treat the problem, but the issue is mainly one of understanding how blisters arise and where they appear.

Blisters are evidence of a tight grip; their location highlights the pressure points. It's easy to fool yourself that your hold is relaxed. Instead, assume that there's no endpoint to reducing unnecessary tension. *Keep inviting ever more release.*

Hooking your fingers loosely around the end(s) of the handle(s), means less tension is created in your wrists, forearms, shoulders, and neck muscles. More power can then be generated in the drive, from your legs and hips, and there is less risk of strain and injury to your lower back, ribs, and forearms.

Frank Cunningham talks of being inspired by the orangutan, whose thumbs are *out of the way* when it swings from branches.

- Our thumbs are *fully opposable* and operate in a different plane to the other fingers.
  - In sculling, the thumbs should make the *lightest* contact around the ends of the handles.
  - On the indoor rower, their rest position during the drive should be *hanging down* beneath the handle, rather than placed on top, or directly behind it.

So, hone your rowing stroke by starting with arms and shoulders only, then you can add in pelvic rock and body swing, before progressing *up the slide* to quarter-slide, half-slide, three-quarter slide and, finally, full slide.

On the way you'll discover the "three halves" of the rowing stroke: that is, towards *each end* of the slide and *in the middle.*

The main aim of this practice is to maximise the length of the stroke, without moving your body or the seat.

Commonly described as "arms only", you should, in fact, engage the shoulders to draw the arms in.

You'll be engaging your "lats" (latissimi dorsi muscles) to add a few extra inches of movement to the shoulders, and to protect the smaller, weaker muscles of the forearms and wrists.

(re-visit Exploration 9: The role of the lats, in Chapter 4.)

1. Arms and shoulders only

Video # 21 View at: www.youtube.com/rowingfromtheinsideout

Although this is an *"Arms and Shoulders"* practice, nothing exists in isolation, so be open to feedback from the rest of your body, while thinking of the drive as actually *starting from the feet*, as described below:

- Start with your legs straight – but knees soft, sitting tall and leaning back a little – holding the handle with your arms extended.
  - Ask your neck to release, so that your head is delicately poised on top of the spine.

- Allow your spine to lengthen itself, supported by the pelvis, and with your deep abdominal muscles engaged.
- Notice if your hold on the handle is relaxed, the ends of your fingers wrapped loosely – close to the ends of the handle – rather than nearer the middle.
- From this condition of poise, begin the drive by pressing the *flats* of your feet into the foot stretcher, avoiding tension in your neck and shoulders.
- At the same time, roll or curl your fingers further around the handle, which lifts slightly. This sets up a connection all the way through the body to the shoulders, which will draw the arms in.

▶ Create a smooth acceleration of the handle through the drive.

- Allow the wrists to flex or arch *upwards,* very slightly. The level of the handle in the drive will be a few inches higher than in the recovery and rises up a little towards the end.
- Imagine the path of the hands like the travel of a bicycle chain, with small cogs at the front and back ends.

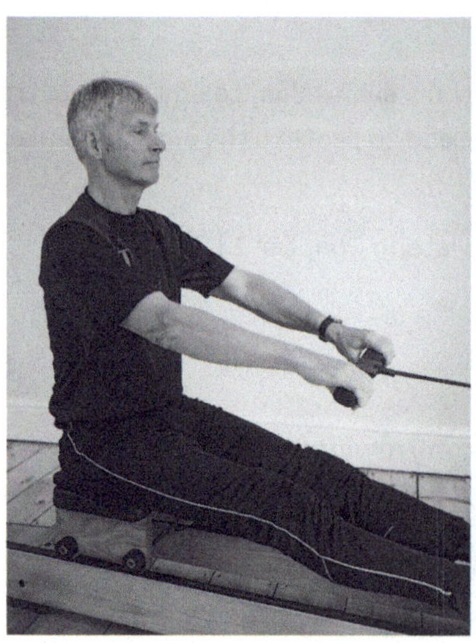

- In the last few inches of the drive:
  - Draw the shoulders fully *back* while rolling out, uncurling or extending the fingers from the main knuckle (metacarpophalangeal) joints – as in a "wood-whittling" or potato-peeling motion.
  - The wrists drop only a little, and then – without delay – *send* the handle a little *downwards* and *away*. The thumbs can lightly touch the lower ribs at the sides, as you do this.
  - *The pull-through sets up the follow-through.* On the *WaterRower,* the thumbs can lightly support the handle on the recovery.
  - As the arms are "flung" away, the shoulders reach *forwards* but *do not lift.*
  - While reaching forwards, allow your spine to elongate; the handle will arrive just above the knees. Stroke rate will be high – close to 40 spm (strokes per minute).

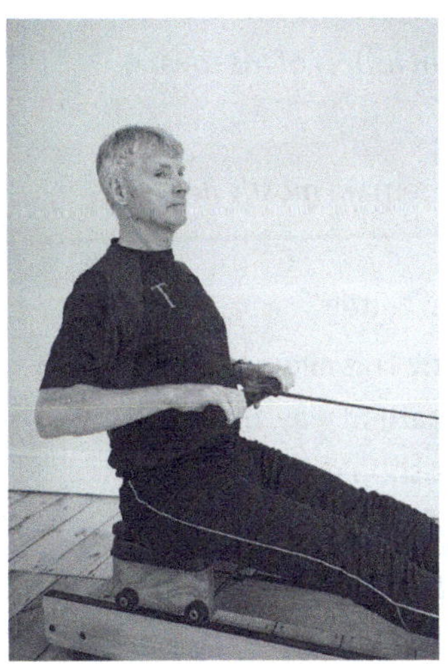

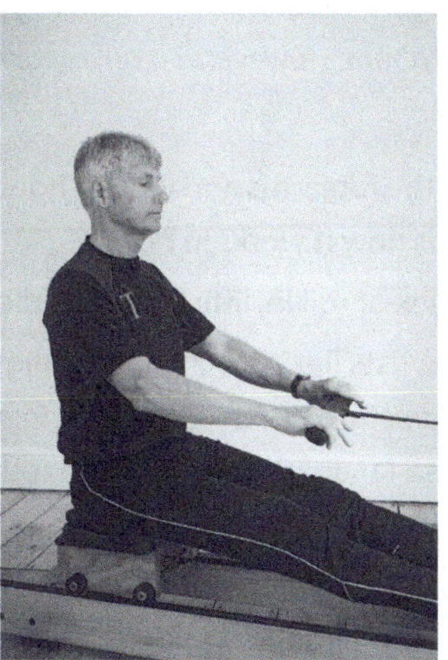

- Pause here for a moment, to review.
  - Frame your intention clearly again, before starting another stroke by pressing your feet on the foot stretcher.
  - A question that's often asked is: *how should the elbows bend – into the sides of the body, or "winging" outwards?*

The answer is – neither one nor the other: just let the elbows find their way *without interfering with the action of shoulders and hands and wrists.*

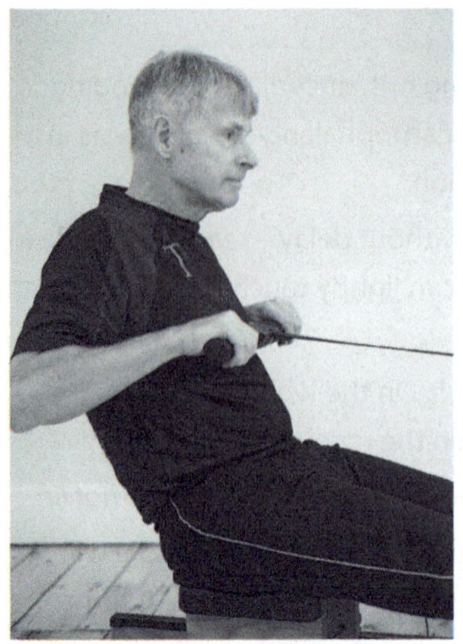

It's commonplace to see competitive rowers – hoping to achieve their highest ergo score in training – arriving at a "give-a-dog-a-bone position": that is, *lying back* way too much by the end of the drive, with the handle arriving as high as the upper chest, the wrists over-flexed, and the elbows pulled into the sides. Not only does this compromise the lower back, shoulders and forearms, but it doesn't work in the boat, so scullers are not doing themselves any favours by practising this movement on the ergo.

Replicating the way the fingers should work in sculling – ***while on the indoor rower*** *– is not usually talked about. However, it is an important aspect of the rowing action, well worth focussing on.*

- In both contexts, while the forearms and wrists should remain *mostly flat* during the stroke, here is how it works in detail:
  - At catch, the fingers flex or roll in, lifting the handle(s) a little.
  - During the drive, the wrists flex or arch *up* very slightly This allows the elbows to draw *back and away* from each other in a natural way, through the arm pull, but not so far apart or upwards that the shoulders tighten or lift.
  - Then, in the release into recovery, the fingers roll *out and down* so that the wrists extend slightly, sending the handle(s) away.
  - The handle again travels in a straight line, a few inches lower than the drive.

2. Arms and shoulders plus pelvic rock and body swing

Video # 22 View at: www.youtube.com/rowingfromtheinsideout

Next, add in the range of body motion available to the rower without the seat moving. The main objective is to extend the length of the drive without bending the knees and – most importantly – without bending the spine at the waist.

This requires some suppleness in the hamstrings. The knees must remain soft: any bracing will tighten the hamstrings, pulling on your lower back.

The other object of this skill practice is to **join the ending of the drive to the beginning of the recovery**.

In standard rowing instruction, the sequence in the recovery is usually characterised as the reverse of the drive: in other words, legs, body, arms in the drive phase are followed by arms, body, legs of the recovery phase. This introduces a "stop" into the main body motion, from swinging backwards to swinging forwards.

In the stroke, which is flowing and connected, the recovery should follow through seamlessly from the drive. Let the arms, then, be sent forwards *as* the body begins its forward swing, rather than waiting for the body to follow the arms. No pause is apparent as the torso changes direction from swinging back, to swinging forward, like the swing of a pendulum. (Try visualising it in an upside-down world, pivoting from below.)

The torso swings from up to 30° of backwards lean – lying a little further back than the previous arms and shoulders drill – to arrive at least close to the vertical, if not achieving a small degree of forward lean, depending on your hamstring flexibility.

As in arms and shoulders previously, the drive should start from the arches of the feet.

- From the next stroke, *driving off the flats of the feet*, work your back *against* your legs, to create the back swing.
  - As you approach no more than 30° of backwards lean – 11 o'clock on a clock face, if you could see yourself from the right – the arms look to be playing "catch up": they trail very slightly behind the swinging back of the torso.
  - The swinging back is arrested by the deep abdominal and pelvic muscles switching on powerfully, and the hollowing of the chest.

- As the shoulders are completing the arm draw, give yourself the idea of *springing up* out of the hips, to start the forward swing. You may notice the seat moves back ever so slightly as the pelvis reverses its tilt.
- Your glutes, quads, deep abdominals, and calf muscles release; think "*widen*" or "*smile*" across the "cheeks" of the buttocks.
- Without delay, this up and over movement of the torso *reverses* the direction of the arms, so that they are flung *forwards and slightly downwards* as the fingers roll out the handle.
- *Reach from the hips towards your ankles.*
- Your stroke rate will be about 30-35spm.

▶ Monitor your lower back to avoid bending from there.

- Flex from the hips but *stop swinging forwards* as soon as you sense your hamstrings beginning to tighten – alerting you to the limit of your forward lean, and so as not to compromise your back.
- Lower your stroke rate to make it easier to notice this.

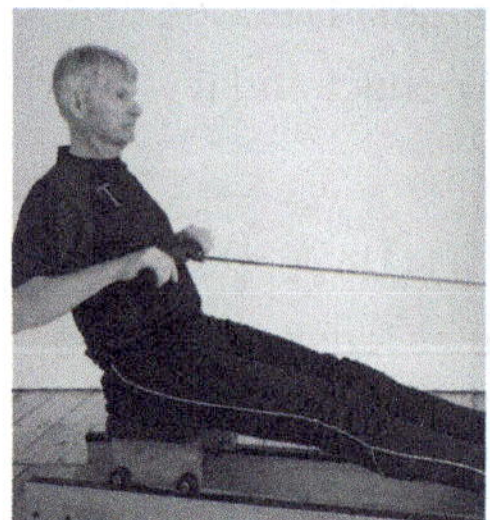
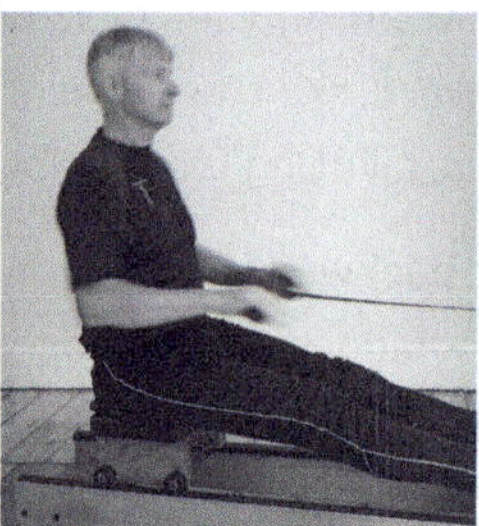

Try doing it badly – with care:

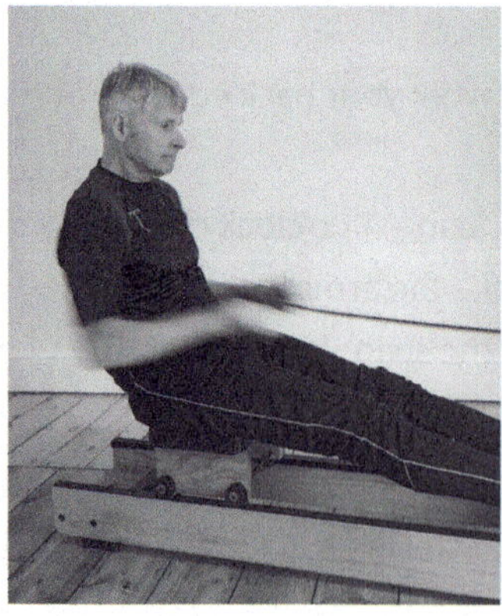

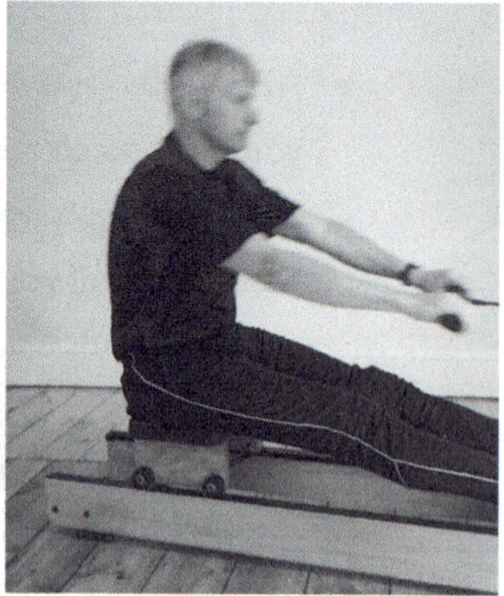

- To do it badly, this time lean back *without* switching on the deep abdominal muscles. You'll go into a slump and lean back way too far.
  - Send the hands away next – conventional rowing instruction – and notice how the back fails to lengthen itself out of its collapse, and that the swing forward, when not energised by the pelvic rock, is quite sluggish.
- Without holding the handle, place the *back of one hand* against your *lower back*, to directly compare the difference between *bending the spine* and *bending from the hips*.

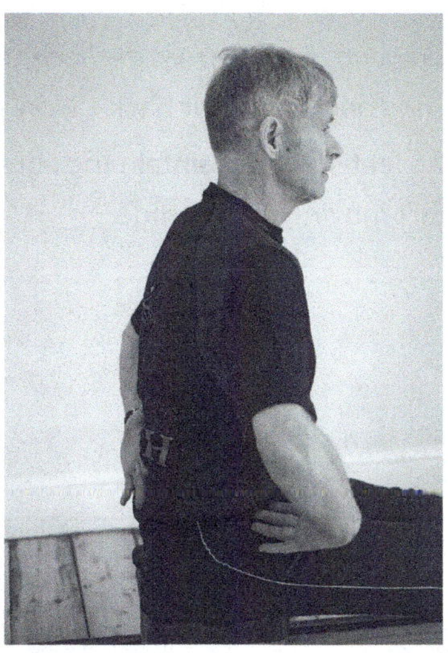

3. Quarter-slide

Video # 23 View at: www.youtube.com/rowingfromtheinsideout

The key skill to be acquired is to begin the journey up the slide **by letting the knees bend after the pelvis rocks over**, which swings the body up and over from the hips.

The weight transfers from towards the back of the sitting bones towards the front, as the pelvis tilts further forwards ("anterior tilt").

Now you are part-way to achieving the full catch position of the torso, where the body is inclined significantly forwards.

The handle arrives **beyond** the knees and **above** the shins **before** the knees begin to "break" or bend.

This is the first of the "three halves" of the rowing stroke.

Notice that the seat may move slightly further backwards, in the transition from the very end of the drive to the beginning of the recovery, before sliding forwards.

In the next stroke, following "*Arms and shoulders plus pelvic rock and body swing*":

- Let the knees rise just a little, after hinging forwards from the hips. Stop moving up the slide when the shins are at an angle of approximately 20-25°.
  - Once more, give yourself permission to pause momentarily, gathering yourself before starting the next stroke.
  - Start the drive by *pressing through from the heels* to the balls of the feet, letting your hips – *and only then* your back – work *against* the legs.
  - On the recovery, the feet should maintain the lightest contact on the foot stretcher, as you start moving up the slide.

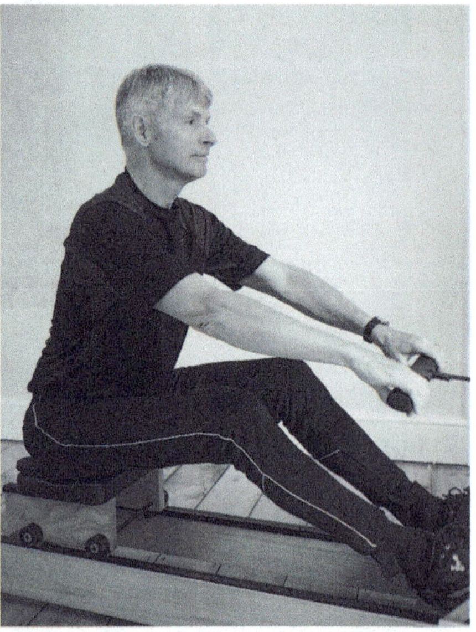

The proper sequencing of the drive should now be much clearer: legs, back and shoulders/arms. And on the recovery, it's body **and** arms, then legs. Once this first of the "three halves" of the stroke is established, progress up the slide should follow readily.

4. Half-slide

Video # 24 View at: www.youtube.com/rowingfromtheinsideout

Hips and knees continue to bend as you approach half slide. Shins will now be at 45°.

The aim is to achieve the body angle which is to be maintained all the way up to full slide, that is, a forward lean of up to 30°; or, viewing yourself from the right – visualising a clock face – the angle of your body should be close to 1 o'clock.

Your "behind" stays behind you, as you approach catch.

Feel the power of the legs and hips really beginning to apply now – their major contribution to the stroke.

5. Three-quarter slide

Video # 25 View at: www.youtube.com/rowingfromtheinsideout

As the seat continues sliding forwards, is it possible to maintain the same angle of the body?

It should remain the same as the lean achieved at half slide. Shins will now be at an angle of 65° or so, by three-quarter' slide.

- Feel the weight on the sitting bones lighten as you press your heels onto the foot stretcher, at the same time rolling your fingers.
  - Then pay attention to the hips, so that handle and seat start moving back together, and at the same speed ("coupling").
  - Without delay, the back begins swinging back and there'll be more pressure on the balls of the feet.
  - As quarter-slide approaches, the shoulders *start* reeling in the arms – and only then do they *begin* to bend.
- Cut short the arm action and return to three-quarter slide.

This is the middle half of the "three halves" of the rowing stroke.

- Remember, don't open your back until ***after*** the seat and handle have coupled.
  - And don't start to "break" the arms until close to the end of your aborted drive.
  - As the sequence unfolds, the various parts of the movement should begin to integrate smoothly.
- Finally, row the whole stroke – completing the drive – and don't stop at quarter-slide.

Try doing it badly, where seat and handle don't move at the same speed at the start of the drive (poor "coupling"):

- Give yourself permission to go wrong, by opening your back too early: Start the push-off from the balls of the feet, instead of the heels.

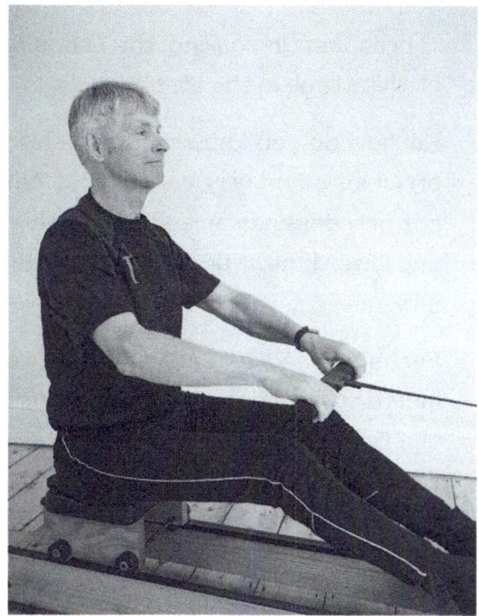

- Alternatively, try to open the back as soon as the heels go down; this is harder to do because getting the heels down first tends to *prevent* the back opening early.
- So, if the back opens too early, the drive from the legs is subverted, less power is generated, and the lower back is impacted.

6. Full slide

Video # 26 View at: www.youtube.com/rowingfromtheinsideout

The final objective is to achieve the longest stroke possible – using Fairbairn's words – "without reaching beyond the strong point of the back".

The secondary objective is **to not to bend the arms by pulling prematurely** – but to use them to lever the transmission of power, by driving first of all with the legs, and then working the back.

Maximum "compression" will be achieved by full slide. But the question is, what is to be compressed? Many rowers round their backs into a pronounced C-shape.

To be sure, the more the legs bend, the more the spine must "gather" or flex – somewhat. However, as full slide is approached, the aim should be to preserve as much length in the spine as possible. The torso will be at its ▸

◀ broadest: in sculling, the hands have moved to their widest separation at this stage in the stroke cycle.

So, how do you know when you have reached full slide? Rowing coaches often insist on vertical shins at catch, a 90° angle. The ability to do this not only depends on ankle flexibility, but also the relative lengths of upper and lower legs: if upper legs are much longer than lower legs, this may be difficult.

Perhaps a more realistic aim is to *approach* the vertical, rather than insisting on achieving it. In some boats you can change the angle of the foot stretcher, as well as its height. With the indoor rower, raising the foot stretcher will compensate for some ankle inflexibility, but the downside is that it will be harder to reach from the hips. Conversely, by lowering the foot stretcher, more forward lean at catch is achieved, so that more weight can be transferred to the feet to generate a more powerful stroke. Balancing one factor against the other is a trade-off.

If you notice that one heel starts to rise before the other, it means that one ankle is stiffer. If so, stop there – don't continue up the slide until the heel of the more flexible ankle lifts: you've already reached your full slide before that. If that signal is ignored, the back will start to twist, again risking injury: the stroke needs to be as close to perfect symmetry as possible.

So, when the heels begin to lift off the foot stretcher, you'll know when you've reached *your* full slide. They are your internal "front stops" – the physical checks on the slides in the racing shell, which limit how far the seat can slide forwards.

Only allow the heels to rise by a few millimetres. If they lift more than that, your "behind" will no longer be behind you: as it slides underneath you, you'll be sitting on your lower back, compressing the spine – even more so as the drive gets underway – risking serious injury. And the stroke will be much weaker.

Try doing it badly:

- As you approach catch, continue to slide the seat forward.
  - It will now arrive underneath the shoulders, your "behind" will no longer be behind you, and the heels will leave the foot stretcher.
  - Shins may be at more than a 90° angle.

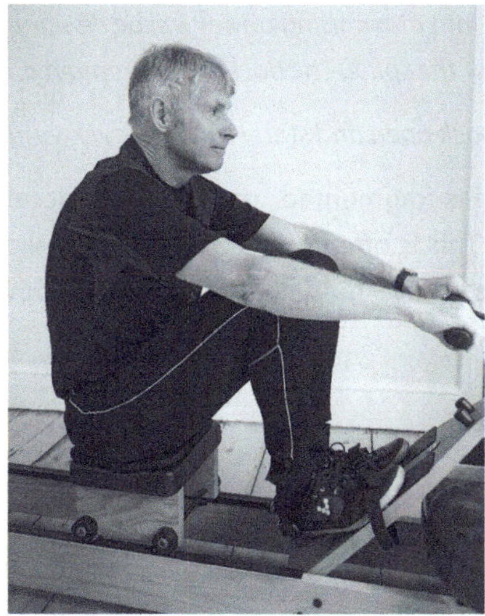

- Next, try stretching your arms further forward – this is what elite rowers often do, when over-lengthening their stroke – and see if you can feel what is happening:
  - Are you still reaching from the hips, or are you bending from your back?
  - Try to sense even small degrees of this over-reaching.

Reaching beyond what Steve Fairbairn called the "strong point of the back" risks hurting it. Scullers lurching into the catch disturb the run of the boat, and the blades tend to "sky" before being dropped too deeply into the water.

Energy that should go into maximising power will be dissipated, in taking out some of the excessive curve of the spine. The back should remain firm and "stacked up".

But when should the back open and start swinging backwards?

If delayed, the stroke is fragmented, and a smooth acceleration through the drive is not possible. This is often called "shooting the slide" or "bum-shoving", where the seat moves back faster than the handle, and power is lost.

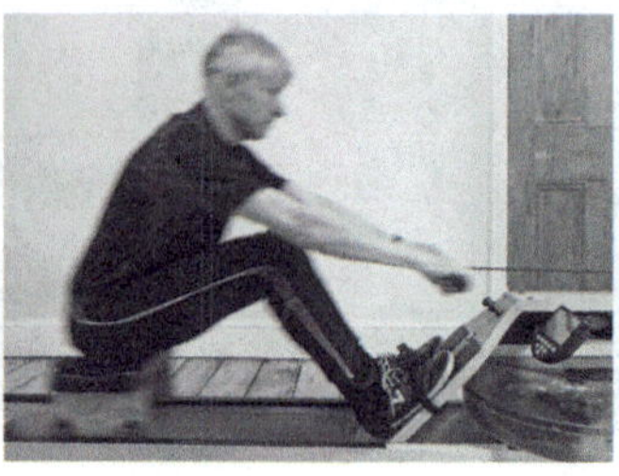
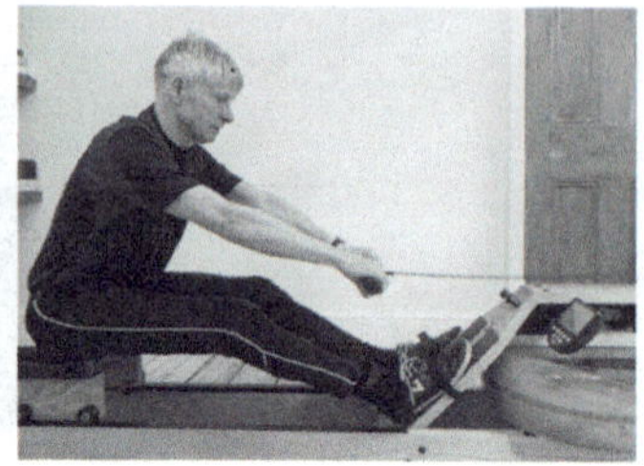

What is extraordinary is that this is used as a drill by coaches, to seek to avoid the back opening too early. However, a possible unintended consequence is to condition the elite rower to expect back pain as a consequence of their rowing.

So, use this movement *only* as "error correction", that is, repeat it no more than two or three times, to identify what should be avoided at all costs.

Some coaches say that the back comes into play at half-slide, when shins are at 45°. Perhaps the exact timing is a matter of "feel", balancing the relative strength of legs, back, shoulders and arms, which will govern – in the individual rower – precisely at what point the next part comes into play. As the hips move *back* and the spine *lengthens*, the back starts to work *against the hips* and contributes significantly to the strength of the drive.

Driving off the heels, and "coupling" the movements of the seat and handle(s), ensures that the back neither opens prematurely nor too late by "shooting the slide".

- At catch position, play with weight transfer from sitting bones to heels and back again as you commence the drive, the handle moving synchronously with the seat. Quickly interrupt the drive, sending the handle away to recover.
  - Move the seat only a few inches for this drill.
  - The arms do not bend. The deep shoulder muscles (the "lats") activate.
  - Do not apply any power to start with, just explore the transition from three-quarter slide to full slide, and back.

- Moving back and forth, through this small distance, the legs will tire quickly, so don't overdo this practice.

This is the final one of the "three halves" of the rowing stroke.

Practise these drills that elite rowers constantly re visit. Never lose sight of them – but approach them mindfully: use clarity of intention to refine the quality of movement and your experience of the essential elements of the rowing action.

To return to the "conscious competence" model once more – the process is similar to learning to drive a car. Progress from "conscious incompetence" to "conscious competence" to "unconscious competence".

In other words, in due course your muscle memory will start to take over. You won't have to obsess over the small details, which will tend to take care of themselves.

However, if you want to continue to improve, adopt the "zen mind, beginner's mind attitude". Check from time to time if you are actually doing what you want to be doing; get video feedback. Be humble and constructively critical. Loop back to "unconscious incompetence" and see what you find. And then move forward again.

Now that the recovery phase has been completely "unpicked", and you know what happens at each end of the slide – and in the middle – you are ready to go deeper into the whole stroke.

7

The whole stroke...and nothing but

You should feel the well-drawn stroke
as a single surge of energy...
not produced by a succession of separate
efforts by the legs, back and arms.

Frank Cunningham

Joel Roger's iconic photo of Frank Cunningham in 2004, capturing the initiation of the drive.

Notice, amongst other things, his loose hold on the handles, relaxed face and steady gaze into the distance; and the start of the "one cut": the instantaneous slicing of the blades into the water as the feet are pressed down.

In the previous chapter, the rowing stroke was divided up to explain how each part should work in relation to the whole. The process of focussing on particulars – and then reshaping the totality – never stops, for it is the only way to develop your rowing to its highest level.

It also means that rowing should never become boring for you. I have, on occasion, tried listening to music or a podcast while on my *WaterRower*. However, I found I'd rather not be distracted and pulled away from the experience of being fully in my body and connecting to the responsiveness of the equipment.

On this journey, new insights come your way. Subtle adjustments take place, and from time to time your rowing takes a quantum leap. As more and more of the nuances of rowing are revealed – and your thinking clarifies – the quality of the whole stroke is transformed from within.

No-one now disputes the order of events in the drive sequence: legs, body and finally arms, come into play. From today's perspective, it can seem almost incomprehensible that, in the early years of the introduction of the sliding seat, rowers were so wedded to rowing on a *fixed* seat that the body and arms still initiated the drive, with legs only joining the party later.

By the very end of the recovery, major muscle groups – the quads, glutes, calves and lats – are under stretch, each primed to contract strongly.

The previous chapter took you to the point where, poised at catch – and ready to begin the drive – the "single surge of energy" that Frank Cunningham describes can be unleashed.

All parts of the body come into play – in sequence and altogether – to make the drive essentially one movement, a continuous flow of energy in the body, with no interruption at any point.

This invites the question: how does energy then flow through into recovery, if the cyclical process is to renew itself?

Tai-chi, power generation and the circuit of energy in the body

Tai-chi and AT complement each other. Both use awareness and intention to inform body movement. FM Alexander directed much of his attention to his neck and head, because of the vocal issues hampering his acting career.

Tai-chi, at root a martial art, is concerned with generating power in fighting. This power is "borrowed" from the ground via the arches of the feet. Shortly you'll understand precisely where the "power points" are – in the heels – and how this leads to a sequence in the feet which underlies the order of the drive.

This insight pinpoints, I believe, exactly what Cunningham was advocating – when he said to start the drive by springing off the "flat of the feet" – and links to Hanlan's claim that the control of the boat lay in his feet.

Video # 27 View at: www.youtube.com/rowingfromtheinsideout

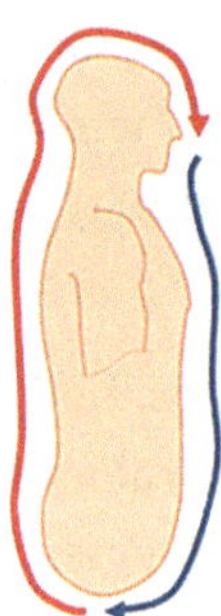

According to the Chinese Way of Taoism, which influenced Tai-chi, there is a vital circuit of energy in the body, known as the *microcosmic circuit* or *lesser heavenly circulation*. This accords with fundamental principles of the physical universe, of which we are a part.

In the basic microcosmic circuit, energy flows *up* the spine to the crown of the head, and then travels *down* the front of the body to the perineum (the pelvic floor). It then returns back up the spine, and so on.

If there is no stiffness or tension in the body, this energy can flow easily out into the limbs and back again. This is known as the *macrocosmic* or *greater heavenly circulation*.

- *Rowing in slow motion, tune in to and see if you can identify these subtle aspects of the rowing action*:
  - *At the beginning of the drive, or "connection"*, energy travels *up* from the feet through the legs, and *up* the spine to the head; and finally, as the arms are reeled in by the shoulders at the end of the drive, energy moves *down* the front to the perineum.
  - *In the release* – the transition from the end of the drive into recovery – energy then moves back *up* the spine to the head, and *out* through the arms; and then back *down* the front into the feet, by the end of the recovery.
  - And on and on…

What are the connections – between the feet and hands/fingers – that are necessary to produce an effective drive?

The fundamental sequence in the feet

How is the "gesture" of the whole rowing stroke – as Frank Cunningham describes it – supported by the feet?

Towards the end of the recovery, as pressure builds on the balls of the feet, it is very tempting to initiate the drive from there, especially if the range of movement at the ankles is limited.

Cunningham talks, however, about the necessity of driving off the "flat of the feet". This requires waiting until a moment later, when pressure on the heels starts to lighten, and *they begin to lift by the tiniest amount.*

To find and use the "flat of the feet", you must first access your "power points": that is, immediately your heels begin to lighten on the foot stretcher, *get the inside of your heels down*, pressing through to the big toe side of the balls of the feet as the drive accelerates.

The outside edges of the arches of the feet, in turn, make firm contact with the foot stretcher. There is now no danger of falling backwards off the seat – whether in the boat or on the indoor rower – if the balls of the feet maintain their pressure on the foot stretcher right through to the end of the drive.

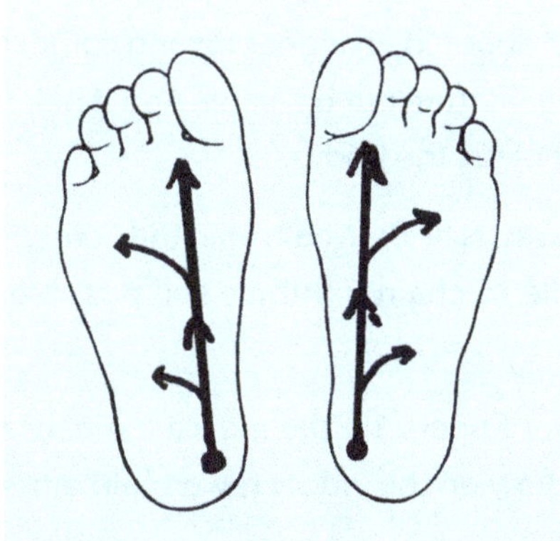

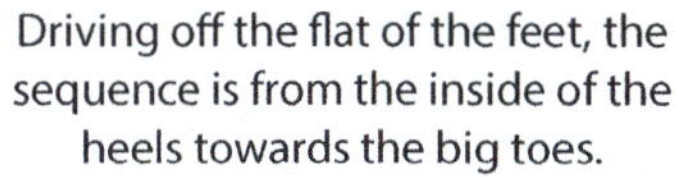

Driving off the flat of the feet, the sequence is from the inside of the heels towards the big toes.

In so doing, the arches load and the rower springs off the foot stretcher.

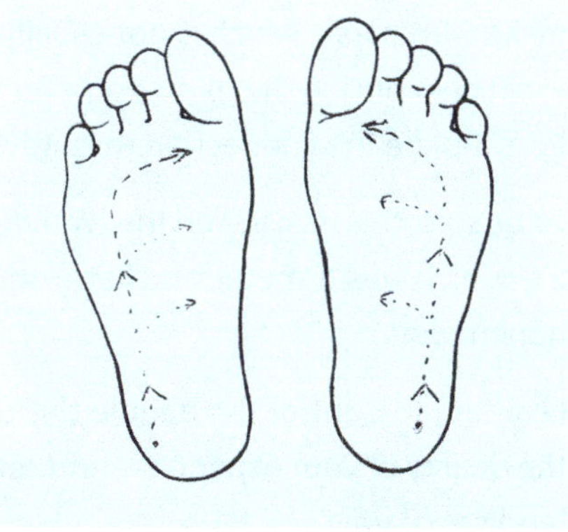

In the recovery, the outside edges of the heels rest lightly first, rolling through the outside edges of the balls of the feet so that the whole surface of the the feet lies flat (pronating), pressure building up on the balls of the feet.

At release, there is a moment of stillness of the body as the backward swing comes to a stop, while the forward swing takes over.

As the rower comes up out of the pelvis, the feet appear to hover over the foot stretcher, but maintain the lightest contact with it. The pelvis goes into anterior tilt and the hamstrings, previously under stretch, contract, and help draw the body up the slide on the indoor rower, while the boat glides underneath the sculler.

As the recovery proceeds, the feet – pronating (as in walking) – lay themselves back down on the foot stretcher, starting with the *outside edges of the heels*, through to the *little toe sides of the balls of the feet*, and finally the *insides of the balls of the feet*.

A handle on the erg and oarsmanship

One theme of this book is to highlight the commonality of being on the erg and being in a racing shell.

In rowing, *blades* refers to the ends of the oars that "catch" the water. The skill of oarsmanship – how to control the blades in and out of water – can obviously only be learnt properly in a boat.

However, replicating as far as possible the movements the fingers and hands make with oars – which is not usually talked about in an indoor rowing context – can help bridge the gap if you ever want to venture out on water. And it helps to complete the connection through the whole of the body.

To be sure, this is easier on the *WaterRower* with its flexible belt, than the *Concept 2* – which has a metal bracket from handle to chain – but it's still possible, nonetheless.

Learning to control the handle through your fingers, on the erg, can enhance the quality of your experience and sense of flow on the indoor rower: Fairbairn's "endless chain".

It's often said that the wrists should remain entirely flat through the stroke, but this is a recipe for stiffness. There should be some freedom of movement at the wrists. At "connection", the fingers roll *in* (flexing) – lifting the hands a little, but not the shoulders – so that, during the drive, the wrists are slightly flexed or arched *upwards*.

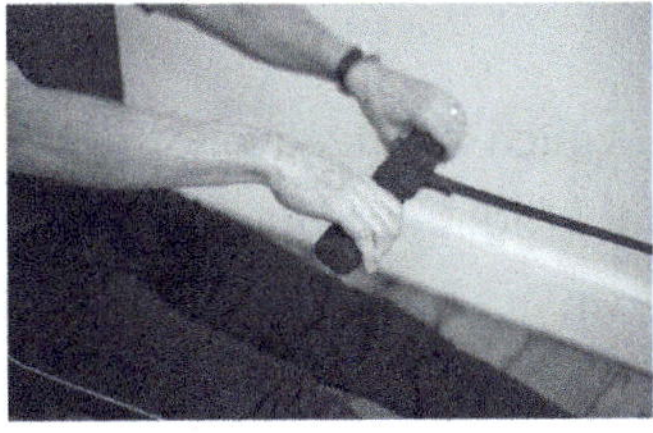 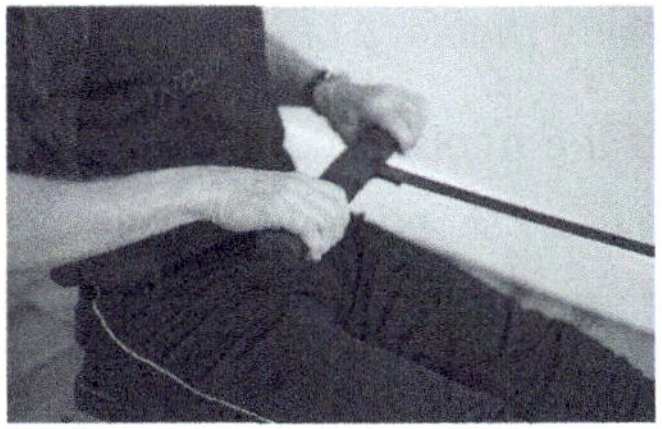 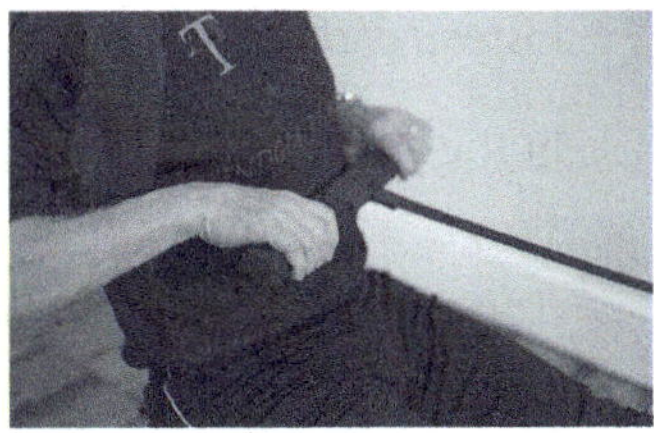

What happens on the water?

The *blades* are *squared* (that is, vertical) during the drive, to maximise their hold on the water to move the boat effectively forward. During the recovery the blades are *feathered* (that is, horizontal), so as to not get caught in the water and to reduce air resistance.

The big question is, how best to manage the transitions, in going from squared to feathered and vice versa? Conventional coaching on the transition from the end of the recovery to drive, holds that the blades should be:

1 Squared early.
2 Then dropped into the water before the feet are pressed down.
3 Finally used to lever the boat forward.

When the blades are put into the water – squared – before being driven through, the boat will be checked more than is necessary.

Frank Cunningham recommends the classic "sculler's entry/catch" as the best solution for reducing boat speed as little as possible when the blades enter the water. At the beginning of *The Sculler at Ease,* he asks the reader to imagine that *"an arm is like an oar"*.

Video # 28 View at: www.youtube.com/rowingfromtheinsideout

- To explore this, visualise (or try) standing waist-deep in a pool, or kneel by a bath full of water through which an arm can be swept.
  - First, play with swishing your hand back and forth on the surface, palm up, as if the blade is feathered.
  - Next, as the arm draws fully back, turn the hand a little *while* dropping it in the water, so that – as the little finger slices in – you can *at the same time* sweep the hand through.
  - Water pressure will "square the hand" if *the arm is relaxed.*

Instead of three separate actions, there is a unitary action.

In the boat, as the inside of the heels are pressed down – which is a relatively slow action – the blades are to be sliced in with a relaxed hold, "lightning quick". *(Look again at the photo of Cunningham).* The blades will square under water pressure and not "crab" (dive deep), when driven through horizontally.

Sherri Cassuto's video on You tube[1] shows her skill in effecting what she calls the "flip catch". She doesn't miss any water: one moment the blades are feathered, the next moment they are buried – now you see them, now you don't!

Also view this historic footage of the Thames Waterman stroke of Frank Cunningham[2,3]. It's of poor visual quality, but you can still clearly see the beauty of his oarsmanship.

If you are used to squaring early – as I was constantly told to do – it can feel very scary at first. The stability of a racing shell consists in keeping the oars approximately level. You could flip the boat if one oar were to dive deeper than the other. However, little by little, confidence grows that the blades will – with the help of water pressure – find the right depth, *if the hold on the handles is relaxed.* And the shoulders are much less likely to lift and tighten as a consequence.

Conventional rowing thought often refers to the removal of the blades from the water as "tapping down" or "extraction" – which could put you in mind of a challenging visit to the dentist! It talks of the blades being:

1 Driven all the way through, squared until the very end of the drive.
2 (Abruptly) lifted to clear the water, still squared.
3 Finally turned onto the feather.

Again, that is, three separate actions.

Return to the simulation of sweeping an arm in water like an oar. As the hand reaches its limit of horizontal travel, wouldn't it feel most natural to *slice* the hand out of the water?

In the simulation, this is best achieved by rotating the forearm – with the thumb leading the turn so that the little finger leaves the water first – and the hand changes direction while beginning its recovery over the surface.

So, just as the natural motion of the hand entering the water for the catch is a unitary action – slicing in and squaring up under water pressure – why wouldn't the exit of the blades from the water also be a single process?

In the boat, wouldn't it be better to secure an easy release by starting to turn the handles – and therefore the blades – at the very last moment of the drive, while maintaining pressure on the water, so that little speed is lost?

The blades will then slice out at an angle of approximately 60° and, while turning completely onto the feather, will already be starting on the return journey of the recovery.

*It's a curvilinear motion, instead of separate box-like actions added together at each end of the stroke. George Pocock, father of Stan Pocock – Frank Cunningham's close colleague – coined the phrase "**one cut**", to encompass this integrated action of the whole stroke: the blades slicing in, then through, and then slicing out of the water.*

How are the blades to be turned at the release?

Via the handles, which means that the fingers need to roll out or extend, to accomplish this. As the work of the legs and back are coming to an end, the shoulders reel in the arms; and, in the last two or three inches of the arm draw, the fingers must do the business, the wrists only dropping a little as the hands are flung downwards and away.

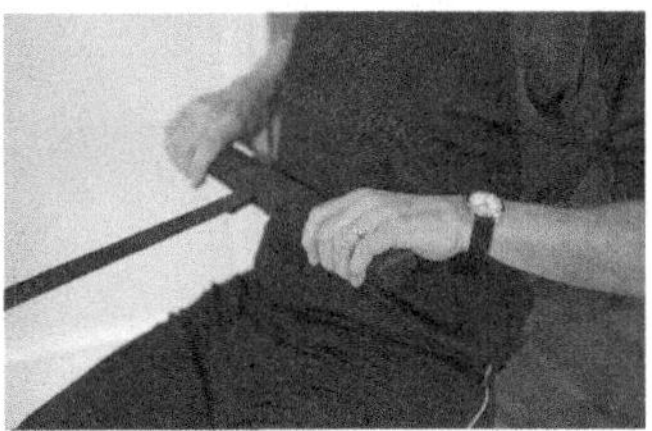

In the boat, the fingers can be extended almost completely, and the weight of the hands counterbalances the oars in the rowlocks, so that the blades stay just clear of the water.

With the *WaterRower,* the handle on its return may need to be supported by thumbs placed lightly underneath.

Try this from time to time to improve subtlety of control of all the fingers:

- To start the drive, as the feet are pressed onto the foot stretcher, at the same time quickly curl the fingers around the handle *one by one* – starting with the little fingers – all the way through to the forefingers.
- In the recovery, roll out the fingers in turn, starting with the forefingers, all the way through to the little fingers.

On the indoor rower, therefore, the flexion and extension of the fingers at each transition can at least partially replicate the manipulation of the oar handles in sculling.

The fundamental connection: from inside of heels to handle(s) to hips

Do you remember rehearsing the beginning of the drive in *Exploration 10* in chapter 4? How did it work for you?

When *hanging off door handles*, as described, did you experience that delicious, spontaneous rise from a squat? If not, perhaps this time, putting your attention into the "power points" – the *insides* of the heels – will make all the difference: access the whole of the arches of the feet, which are put under elastic stretch. Energy can then travel up through the rest of your body.

Cunningham talks about "springing off" the foot stretcher – not stamping on it.

Why do rowing coaches generally not question the wisdom of their athletes pushing off first with the toes or balls of the feet? Ankle stiffness is often part of the issue – and should be addressed (see the stretching exercises in chapter 9).

However, if *rowing is a bending and lifting action in a horizontal plane*, as suggested earlier, trying to lift from the balls of the feet does not make sense: weightlifters get their heels firmly down, to maximise power.

A whole host of unwanted things can follow if you push off the balls of the feet.

- The neck tends to stiffen, and the head retracts.
- The back is likely to open up too soon, and power is lost from the legs.
- It is tiring on the calves.
- The balls of the feet tend to lose their connection to the foot stretcher towards the end of the drive. The rower collapses backwards, affecting the run of the boat as the bow dips.
- Hip flexors then contract to drag the hips forward on the recovery, undermining the forward lean at catch.

So instead, as you approach the catch, make an instantaneous connection from the inside of the heels to the handle(s), to the hips. "Ricochet" your attention as follows:

- As your heels begin to lighten, get the inside of the heels down, to get your weight onto the flat of the feet.
    - Feel the sitting bones lighten on the seat. Take care not to lift right off the seat – you may find it is no longer there when you need it!
- At the same time, roll your fingers lightly around the handle, which lifts slightly.
    - You will now be "hanging your weight on the handle(s)".
    - Your shoulders do not rise but your deep shoulder (latissimus dorsi) muscles activate.
    - Everything is primed and connected.
- Send your attention to the hips, which are driven back and away from your feet.
    - Handle(s) and seat start moving back at the same speed – "coupling".

You have re-visited the last of the "three halves" of the rowing stroke.

From heels to handle(s) to hips to back

Next, the back needs to come into play. As it elongates, let it work against the legs.

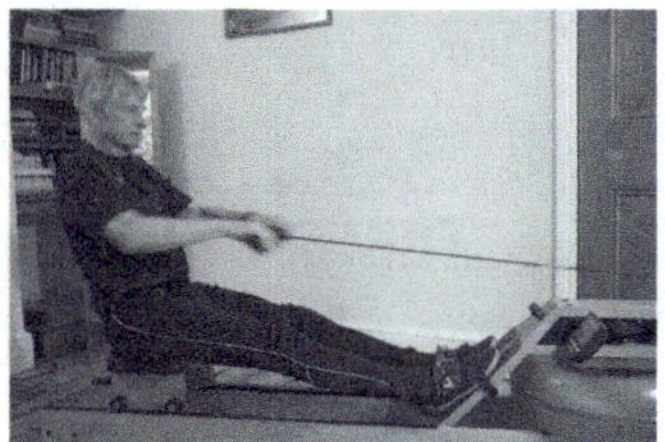

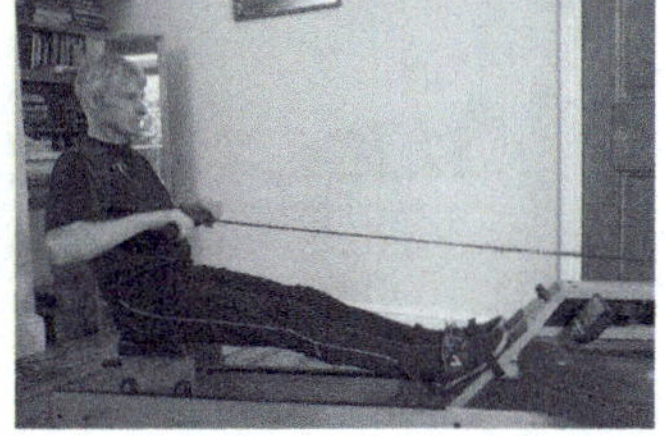

From heels to handle(s) to hips to back to shoulders to arms

Finally, as the power of the previous segment – the back swing – is diminishing, the arm draw makes its contribution to the surge of energy towards the end of the drive. And don't forget the role of the shoulders, drawing back, that reel in the arms.

I pointed out, in the introduction, that what separates the average recreational user on the indoor rower – from the on-the-water rower – is the absence of body swing.

What differentiates the *complete* rower is that there is no apparent delay before the body's forward swing takes over from the backward swing: the movement of an inverted pendulum – the skill that the legendary sculler, Ned Hanlan, exemplified.

And now, once more, the whole stroke...and nothing but

Follow across the double page spread.

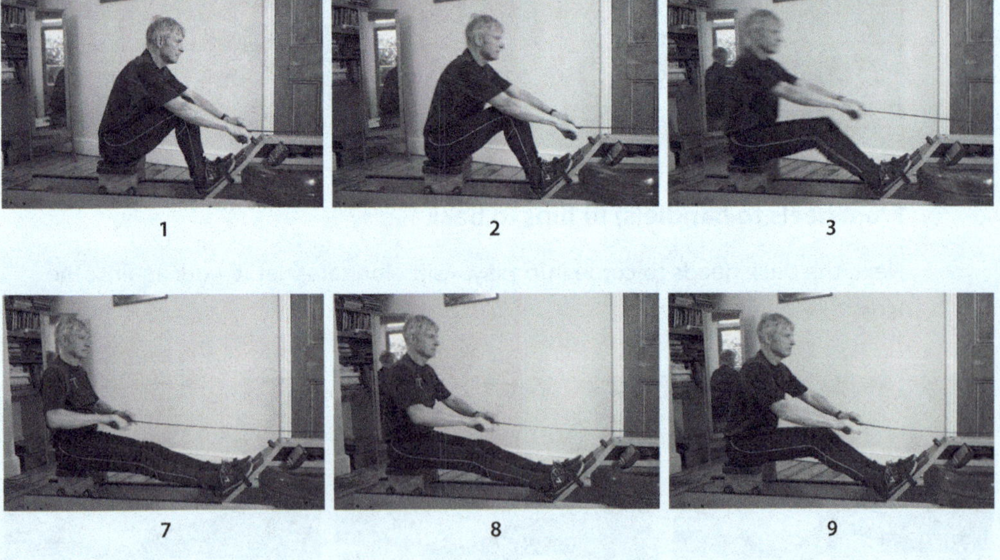

1 2 3

7 8 9

While the shoulders are retracting fully, and the fingers are releasing the blades from the water, the body has already reversed direction up out of the hips, flinging the arms forward:

- *The up-flow in the spine sends an out-flow to the arms.*

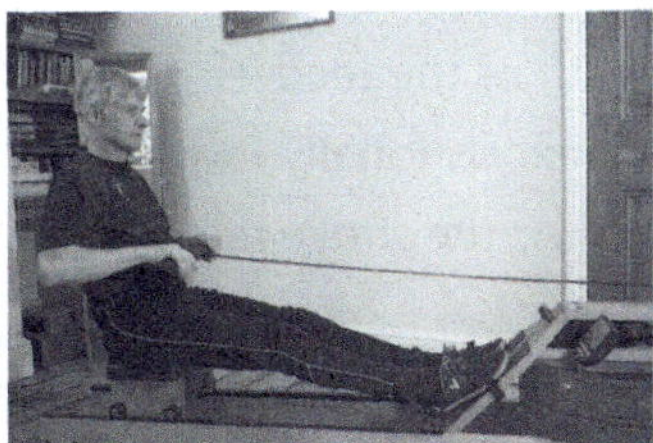
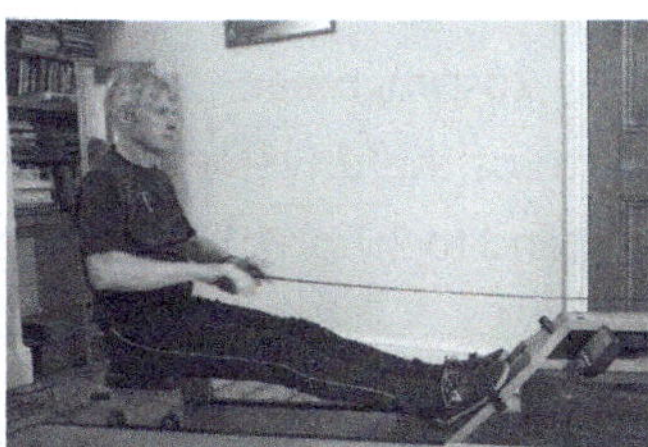
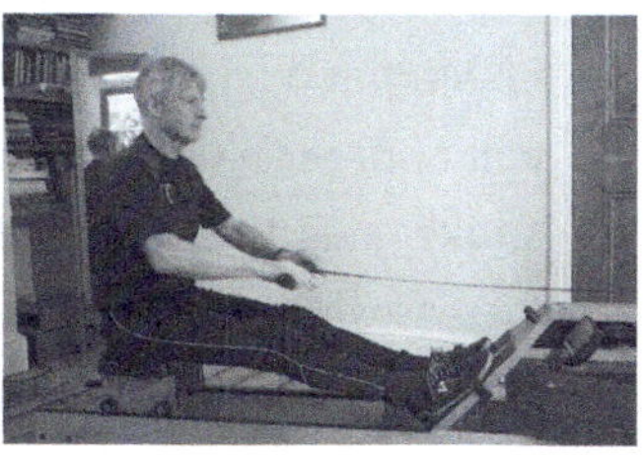

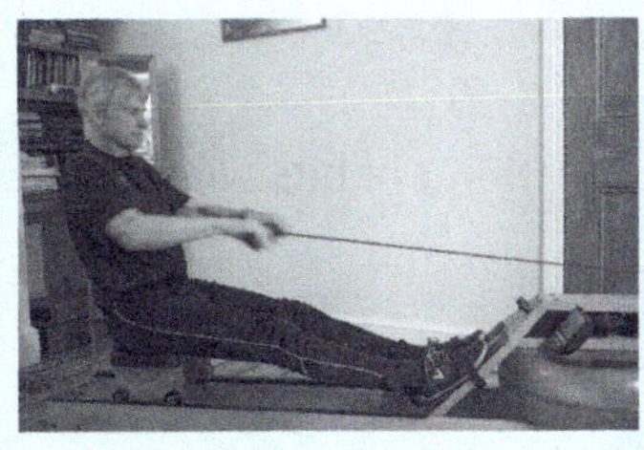
4

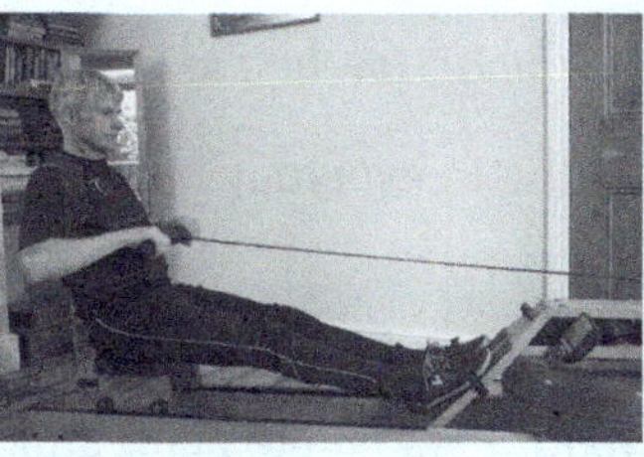
5

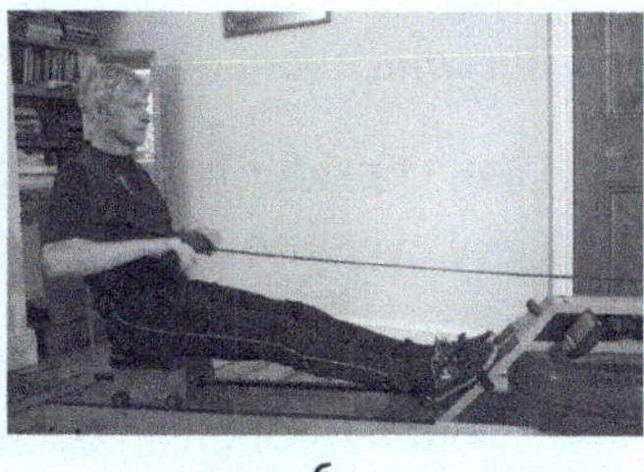
6

10

11

12

Ratio and rhythm

Beginners on the indoor rower tend to rattle up and down at much the same speed, in each direction. Rowing a boat like that, though, would cause it to lurch and lose way. It's also very tiring – muscles will not recover so readily – and the connection/catch will not be so effective. The recovery needs to be at least a little longer than the drive, reflecting their different functions.

Rowing at a leisurely pace, say 20spm, means that the length of the recovery will approach twice the length of the drive: a 2:1 ratio. At exceptionally low stroke rates, the ratio could extend to 3:1 or 4:1, or even more. As the stroke rate increases, it may come close to 1:1.

Maximum speed in the boat is achieved early in the recovery, and the idea is not to interfere with the free running of the boat underneath you.

On the indoor rower, use as little muscular work as possible to bring the seat – and you – back up the slide, ready for the next stroke. The rocking-over of the pelvis, putting hamstrings under stretch, leads to their natural contraction and easy movement up the slide.

Breathing

The case for rowing as a mindful activity, where achieving harmony of mind and body is the main purpose, is the theme of this book.

But what about the role of breathing? How best to breathe?

First, consider how you breathe in everyday life. Those breathing habits will carry over into exercising.

- Anxiety can lead to breathing too quickly and shallowly in the upper chest, often through an open mouth, leading to panic attacks.
- At other times, when concentrating on a task, prolonged breath-holding may occur, often followed by gasps for air when breathing re-starts.

Rowers sometimes cram two breaths into each rowing cycle. There may be little option if you are reaching your limits, but in most circumstances the rate and depth of your breathing will tend to increase comfortably in line with stroke rate. Even top sculler Manson, rating close to an extraordinary 40spm for a large part of his record-breaking race, managed on just one breath per stroke.

Now, exactly how should the breath be synchronised with the stroke cycle? When to breathe in, and when to breathe out?

An Olympic gold medallist in the single sculls, who now runs rowing training programmes, has advocated *exhaling* on the recovery, *inhaling* on the drive:

> *Absolute relaxation occurs through exhaling. With loose lungs, hanging off the leg drive is natural. As the acceleration progresses and the upper body swings open, the lungs fill with air and provide a strong finish position.*
>
> *Some rowers breathe in on the recovery and exhale at the finish. This leads to a shorter stroke length and early use of the upper body. At the finish (when exhaling) the posture "crumbles" in the lower back, and usually knees buckle, instead of staying straight to connect through the foot board.*

He could also have argued – since the recovery lasts longer than the drive – that it may be more comfortable to go for a longer out-breath and a shorter in-breath, which is the case when breathing quietly.

Does this accord with your breathing rhythm?

*The case for the opposite breathing rhythm, **in** on the recovery and **out** on the drive, however, has much to commend it:*

1. Muscles will be oxygenated just before their maximum work.
2. The torso, inflated like a balloon at catch, stays firm in transmitting most of the power from the leg drive; the body is then set up in exactly the same way that weightlifters perform a dead lift.
3. Towards the end of the drive, as the arm draw commences, the abdominal muscles contract more strongly, naturally squeezing out air. They actually stabilise the lower back – contrary to the assertion above – making it easier to then release more quickly up out of the hips to start the movement up the slide.
4. Most athletes breathe *out* as they make maximum effort: for example, witness the grunting of tennis players as they strike the ball. Notice Manson's cheeks puffing out as he completes the drive.

Meditate on the breath

One of the many joys of rowing is to experience its rhythmical activity, especially when breathing in harmony with the flow of the stroke.

Patrick McKeown – in his books *The Oxygen Advantage*[4] and *The Breathing Cure*[5] – explains how to breathe more efficiently and naturally, both in everyday life and while exercising.

This actually entails breathing *less* than you might believe, because over-breathing incurs energy costs from moving more air than is required to maintain blood oxygen saturation. And if too much CO_2 is blown off, O_2 adheres more tenaciously to the haemoglobin in the red blood cells and is not available for producing energy.

McKeown also argues that we should use our nostrils for both in- and out-breaths. Nasal breathing has a direct link to the diaphragm, drawing air deeper into the lungs, where the blood supply is more concentrated. Mouth breathing leads to lifting the upper chest. We are the only mammal – apart from dogs, who regulate their body temperature by panting – that fall into the habit of mouth breathing. And, if the mouth is open, incoming air is not warmed, moistened, and filtered, meaning less protection for the delicate tissues of the lungs.

Recent evidence shows that nitric oxide (NO), produced in the paranasal sinuses and drawn deeply into the lungs in nasal breathing, has a dual role in increasing blood flow and in protecting against harmful micro-organisms. More NO is released during moderate exercise compared with either low or high intensity training, and breathing out through an open mouth, as rowers commonly do – puffing out air – leads to 40% more moisture being lost than if the mouth remains closed.

- So, in rowing, as the arms bend towards the end of the drive, contraction of the abdominal muscles is accompanied by the chest hollowing and the ribs drawing inwards and downwards:
  - Air is naturally squeezed out and, with the mouth closed, echoes quietly the *whooshing* of water in the tank of the W*aterRower.*
  - In sculling, the hands describe the narrowest loop of a figure of 8 (viewed from above), arriving close to the sides of the ribs drawn inwards and downwards.
- During the recovery, when rising out of the hips, the spine elongates and recovers much of its length as it commences its forward lean.
  - The breath stays out for a moment and, as the rower approaches catch, the chest broadens to its maximum – expressed in sculling by the splaying of the arms to their widest point in that figure of 8.
  - Air quickly fills the vacuum in the lungs– upper chest first, then lower down next – the ribs expanding sideways and lifting.

- All the while, the spine maintains as much length as possible. Smile as you approach catch, not only to release acquired tension, but also to open the nasal passages as part of the widening and releasing going on throughout the body.

- It can be tempting to let the air out as soon as the drive starts. However, the spine is lengthening here, maintaining expansion of the chest.
  - So it is better to *delay the outbreath* until the arm draw compels it.
  - While the breath remains in, more oxygen can be absorbed (a process facilitated by the build-up of carbon dioxide, from the work of the drive, and the slight delay before the in-breath).

Rowing as meditation

Video # 29 View at: www.youtube.com/rowingfromtheinsideout

One of the best ways of fine-tuning your rowing is to focus on one part of the stroke at a time.

As the whole stroke begins to fall into place, muscle memory takes over and you can focus more effectively on one aspect of your rowing, letting the rest of the stroke – to a large degree – take care of itself.

Next, see if you can add another focal point without losing track of the first. Here are some suggestions to begin with:

- Gazing mainly into the distance (you can still glance at the monitor from time to time), notice:
  - *Rhythm*: is the stroke unrushed and are you giving the recovery its due? The last inch or two of the slide can be the slowest, as you gather yourself to unleash that surge of energy.
  - *Jaws*: are you clenching your teeth?
  - *Shoulders*: are they relaxed at catch?
  - *Hold:* check your fingers are loosely wrapped around the handle. Are you remembering the potato-peeling/wood-whittling movement?
  - *Fingers:* can you let your fingers extend one by one, on the recovery, starting with the forefingers? And can you quickly wrap your fingers around the handle, starting with the little fingers?

  - *At connection*: see if you can "ricochet" your attention, as described earlier, from the inside of the heels, to handles, to hips, to back, and to shoulders drawing in the arms.
  - *Forearms*: placing a mirror directly in front of you, can you see if your arm action is symmetrical? And does the handle maintain its line during each phase of the stroke?
  - *Body swing*: with a mirror set at 45°, can you see your body swing ranging between 11 and 1 o'clock?
  - *Knees*: are they soft as the drive finishes? Do they stay down until the handle passes over the knees? Do they "give" without resistance as the rock-over from the hips starts? Are you reaching from your hips towards the ankles?
  - *Seat*: does it move slightly further back as the pelvis starts tilting forward? And then does it move forward easily as the hamstrings, under stretch following the rock-over, contract?
  - *Spine lengthening*: at a low stroke rate, notice the points in the rowing stroke where your spine is at its longest: just after the back begins to open in the drive, and as you rise out of the hips in the recovery.
  - *Widening:* from buttock cheeks to facial cheeks during the recovery. Can you smile as you approach connection?

- *Check the sequence in the feet*: try focussing on one foot at a time:
  - Drive from the inside of that heel through to the big toe side of the ball of the foot.
  - Hover over the foot stretcher fleetingly at the finish of the stroke…
  - Then rest the outside edge of the heel on the foot stretcher through to the little toe side and feel the pressure building up over the big toe side of the ball of the foot.
  - Wait until the heel begins to lighten on the foot stretcher and then press the inside of that heel down.
  - Then switch your attention to the sequence in the other foot.
  - Finally, attend to both feet together.

- And here are some other areas of focus:
  - *The acceleration of the handle through the drive*, following straight on into recovery: is it smooth or jerky?

- *Breathing*: relish the transitional stages when the breath is neither going out nor coming in – like a wave rising to its peak or flattening to its trough.
- *To practise "sighting" in a boat on the indoor rower*, turn to look back every fifth stroke, first on one side as you begin the recovery, and let your gaze return straight ahead as you approach catch/connection; then try on the other side.
- *Feel the flow of energy in the body.* At a low stroke rate, say 16-20spm – as the recovery begins – tune in to the rise of energy up your spine, and out to your arms.
- Follow it down your front into the feet, at catch.
- Then, during the drive, from your feet and legs to your pelvis, and back up the spine to the crown of your head.
- Towards the ending of the drive, observe it travelling back down your front, as the shoulders reel in your arms.

There are so many aspects to meditate on: the cyclical flow of energy in your body; the rhythmical process of your breathing; and the metaphor of the rowing cycle following the seasons of the natural world:

Autumn – the finish/release: letting go of the glutes and quads, the deep abdominal and calf muscles, with the feet in the lightest contact with the foot stretcher, and the blades slicing out of the water.

Winter – the recovery: developing rootedness again, ready to unleash the stroke.

Spring – connection/catch: springing off the foot stretcher, the blades slicing simultaneously in, the parts of the body working in sequence and all together.

Summer – the drive: uncoiling and expressing all that stored energy, driving the blades through the water.

Now, trust the process. Enjoy whole rowing with a quiet mind. Listen to – and learn from – any cues your body gives you. Allow change to take place in its own time.

8

The no-sweat rowing workout

The promotional image of the new gym user being inducted by a trainer, described in the introduction to this book, shows them both, hunched – seemingly unaware of their body use – fixated on the display monitor of a rowing machine. The message is that *the* way to improve your fitness is to be concerned with the metrics of going faster, or further, or both – and that proper rowing technique does not merit consideration.

Your fitness aims may be more modest, but no less worthy:

- First, moving a little more than you currently do, will be of significant benefit to your health: rowing is one of the most complete ways of exercising.
- Second – and more importantly – by improving the way you move, it's likely you'll want to row more, simply because it feels good! And your fitness levels will naturally improve.

For whatever reason, there are times, nonetheless, when you are lacking energy. Maybe it's best in those circumstances to take it easy and rest, including lying in the AT releasing position, as described in chapter 5. The body has its reasons.

A cautionary tale

A few years ago, a well-known celebrity suffered a serious stroke shortly after exercising on a rowing machine.

He'd been persuaded that very short bursts of highly intensive exercise were beneficial, could fit into a busy schedule, and would be more effective than longer periods of moderate exercise. He had been trying to row 5K in under 20 minutes, a challenging workout for anyone – especially for someone in their 50s, whose lifestyle had been very stressful for some time. In retrospect, he thought that he may already have suffered two mini-strokes in this period.

There are proponents of high-intensity workouts with what might be called the "get it over as quickly as possible" approach to exercise. The implication is that exercise is something unpleasant, to be endured for the shortest possible time.

When mind and body are separated in this kind of way, though, there will be consequences. Is the body just a machine to be whipped into shape and then ignored for most of the time by the superior intellect? And who will have to deal with the downside if what appears to be good advice doesn't work for *you*? Steering a way through what are often conflicting claims of what is and isn't beneficial, for the mind as well as the body, can be confusing. It makes sense to proceed with caution in incorporating a new approach: begin small, and, if it seems helpful after a little time of using it, progress a little more, building it into your lifestyle and *working with* your body's readiness and capacity for change.

The use of a heart monitor

One measurement worth paying attention to, in a workout, is your heart rate. The use of a heart rate monitor/app will show you how heart rate alters in the course of a session.

When I run – even trying to warm up quite slowly – I find that my heart rate often spikes. The relatively smooth rise in heart rate, as a rowing workout gets underway, is testament to how suitable rowing *can* be in challenging and improving cardio-vascular fitness.

The heart monitor is especially helpful when you are new to exercise. It can help keep you in check when you begin to overdo things. Later, the gap between your subjective level of exertion, and the more objective measure of the work you are doing, narrows. With experience you will come to know – within a few beats – how your heart is rating at any moment.

Choose a heart rate monitor with a hi-lo audible signal to identify target range, and one which records the length of time in your training zone, as well as average heart rate. As a rough guide, stay within 65-85% of your maximum heart rate, calculated by subtracting your age from 220. The monitor/ap can make that calculation for you.

If you are relatively unfit, stay within 65-70% of your maximum heart rate, to begin with. For example, a forty-year-old would train within:

[220 – 40 x 0.65 = 117] and [220 – 40 x 0.70 = 126]:
so, a range of 117-126 beats per minute.

Starting out: a "pyramid" workout

There are a wide range of different workout programmes available – and you could design your own.

The parameters to play with are: how fast you row (your stroke rate), how hard you row (pressure or intensity measured in terms of metres per second travelled, calories burnt, or wattage created), and the length of time of your workout.

Remember, while working out, not to lose sight of your "form": is your rowing technique still on track?

One of the simplest and best strategies is to build up gradually, and then taper off gradually. After warming up so that your heart rate is at the lower end of your training zone, a simple beginning pyramid workout, for example, could be:

- Row for two minutes at 18spm (strokes per minute), then another two minutes each at 20spm, 22spm, 20spm, and back to 18spm. So, a total of 10 minutes.

As your body adapts, you could increase the training load in different ways, depending on how much time you have.

For example:

- Spend longer at each stroke rate and/or…
- Increase the intensity – that is, row with more power.
- Raise the stroke rate and then lower it again, for example: 18, 20, 22, 24, 26, 24, 22, 20, 18.
- Build up to – and sustain – a top rating for longer, for example 3 minutes at 26spm.

For most people, the more the body is challenged, the more it will tend to adapt. As your fitness level improves, you will notice that you have rowed further within your training zone, or that your target distance is achieved sooner. An intermediate goal might be to gradually row further by increments of 200/250 metres, up to 5K.

However, it is the case that a small proportion of people are physiologically unable to improve their aerobic capacity. If that's so for you, enjoy what you *can* do, comfortably.

"The no sweat workout" chapter heading is, of course, a contradiction in terms. "No sweat" is intended to remind you not to waste energy, and to focus instead on *ease and economy of movement*. And, while "workout" could imply a lack of joy while "grinding it out" …

- As you dive deeper into the approach suggested in this book, you should find that your workout is more interesting and engaging than mere brute effort.
  - Ensure your room is well-ventilated: use a fan if it's warm, and perhaps row without a T-shirt.
  - With a modest amount of rowing – and no time to shower – you might find, having cooled down, that you can change back into everyday clothes and still feel presentable.

How often should you row?

- It depends on how much time, in your current circumstances, you can realistically set aside for exercising.
  - A good start would be to find time for three sessions a week, lasting around half an hour each, including warming up and cooling down.
  - At the beginning, take more time playing with parts of the stroke, rather than rowing the whole stroke continuously.

Upping the ante

As your stroke rate increases, can you still maintain "form"?

- In other words, does your rowing start to feel – and look – rushed, ragged and jerky?
  - Does the handle get the "grip of death"?
  - Is your breathing laboured? If so, ease off, and perhaps film yourself to see where you might improve technique.
  - Keep revisiting the basics and practise those rowing skills in need of improvement.

- With more experience, well warmed up and with a sound, dependable technique, you may want to push it a little – and see "what comes off the rails".
    - Try increasing incrementally to a racing pace, say 30spm or more, for a short amount of time.
    - Alternatively, do some interval training, where you alternate high intensity work with low intensity work.
    - On the water, for instance, rowers often row hard for 10 strokes and then lightly for 10, and repeat.

Next up is all about how to cool down after a workout, the sorts of stretches that are particularly worth doing and how best to do them.

9

Cooling down and stretching

The body needs a little time to return to a quieter resting state following any workout.

The simplest thing to do is the reverse of warming up: slowly reduce stroke rate and intensity. By 16-18 strokes per minute, your rowing will feel like slow motion.

Monitor the whole stroke. How does it feel now?

- Heart and breathing rates will lower. And the fitter you are, the quicker your heart rate will return to a resting rate.
- The body will quickly metabolise any accumulated lactic acid from your exertions.

If you are mindful of how you row, with good body use – and if it's just a moderate workout – it is not vital to stretch afterwards every time.

Why stretch?

The two main reasons for performing *static* stretches straight after any exercise are to:

1. Lengthen out the muscles and soft tissues which tend to shorten through repeated activity. The most important muscle groups in rowing are quads and glutes, hamstrings and calves.
2. Increase your range of motion so that your body will move with more ease, enabling a longer stroke. It will also reduce risk of injury because more flexible joints will not be stressed to compensate for stiffness in adjacent joints.

How you perform any stretch merits your full attention.

- The soft tissues will be warm after rowing, which is the best time to perform static stretches in order to avoid causing injury.
  - Take care not to stretch beyond mild discomfort. Monitor the whole of your body while stretching, particularly whether your neck is tensing – indicative of too much force being applied.
  - Be patient, gradually increasing the intensity of the stretch for 20-30 seconds. Think "soften" or release.
  - Towards the end of that time, you may find – as the stretch reflex is inhibited – that the soft tissue will give a little more, and you can stretch further.
  - Notice if one side of your body is stiffer than the other. If so, start and finish stretching on that side to recover more balance. Otherwise, as a general rule, stretch twice on each side.

Some range of motion stretches

Hamstrings

Some elasticity in the hamstring muscles is crucial to achieve the pelvic rock-over at the release.

Why are the muscles at the back of the upper thighs often tight, leaving the individual feeling "a bit hamstrung"?

Some people are born with shorter and tauter hamstring muscles, and that must be taken into account. However, this problem is often exacerbated by everyday body use.

For instance, if you stand with a sway back – either with knees bent or locked – the hamstrings will be in a state of constant tension. All the exercise in the world will not get to the root of the problem. And if you are sat too long at a desk, hamstring and hip flexor muscles do not get much of a chance to be lengthened out.

The commonest hamstring stretch is performed standing, with the leg that is to be stretched extended out in front. A major drawback is that it is difficult to avoid stressing the lower back at the same time.

Perhaps a better way to stretch the hamstrings is in the AT releasing position. The lower back is stabilised on the floor and, with the head supported, the neck can be more easily left alone. Aim to improve your flexibility over weeks and months, patiently and with care. You will need a moderate-length scarf or belt, to provide leverage.

- In the AT releasing position, draw the knees in turn towards the chest (as described in Chapter 5), to release tension in your lower back.
  - Then lift one knee and extend the leg. How far can you draw the foot up and over towards your head? If you cannot get close to the vertical, you have tight hamstrings.
  - With the ends of the scarf looped around your fingers, "lasso" your foot just in front of the heel, and then extend the leg.
  - *Direct* the heel out of the hip while pulling your elbows apart, and in the opposite direction to your head. The aim is to draw the leg towards the vertical – and eventually beyond – without compressing the hip joint.
  - The knee should not be "locked", but otherwise the leg is to be as straight as possible.
  - Don't force this stretch: ensure that each side of the pelvis stays flat on the floor and that there is no stress in the lower back.
- You can take this stretch a little further by using a technique called *PNF* (proprioceptive neuromuscular facilitation).

- For about six seconds – while pulling the your leg towards your head using the scarf/belt – oppose the stretch by trying to pull your leg *away* from your head in the opposite direction.
- Then return to static stretching. You should find that the hamstrings will have released further.

To help achieve a more effective compression of the legs at catch/connection, calf muscles and Achilles tendons need to be elastic enough to allow a good range of ankle flexion.

Calves – superficial

- Step close to a wall with your *left* foot.
  - Rest your *right* hand flat on the wall, with the back of your *left* hand against your lower back, and your little finger on your tail bone.
  - Move your *right* foot a little way behind you and let the ball of the foot rest on a small block of wood 2-3cm thick (in shoes with minimal heels), while the heel rests on the floor.

  - You will probably already feel a stretch in the calf muscle.
  - Then lean forward through the ankle joints, letting your front leg bend, passively (don't push into your knee joint).
  - Think "head away from back heel" to increase the lean and the stretch.

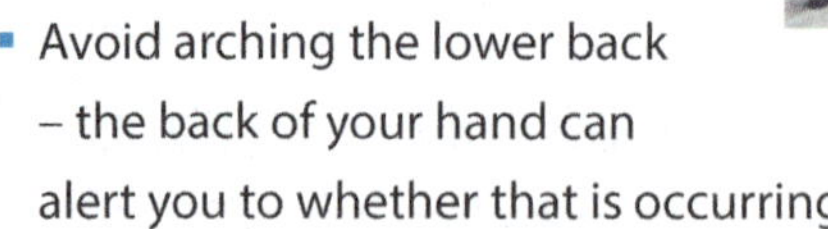

  - Avoid arching the lower back – the back of your hand can alert you to whether that is occurring.

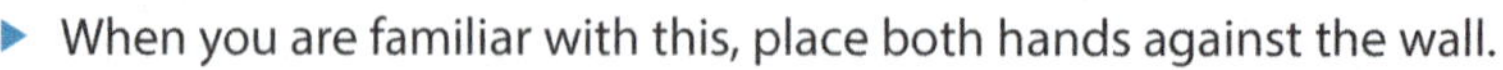

- When you are familiar with this, place both hands against the wall.
- Repeat on the other side.

Calves – deep

- Stand inside a door frame, facing the door jamb.
    - Place one leg *behind* you, bending the knee so the leg is supporting your weight, with the foot slightly turned out.
    - Place the ball of the *front* foot, as high up as you can get it, against the door jamb, and then rest the heel on the floor. Bring your hands lightly around the door frame.
    - Think tall and *very slowly* straighten your back leg.
    - As your weight shifts little by little forwards, the intensity of the stretch in the deeper calf muscle and Achilles tendon will increase.
- Repeat on the other side.

After-rowing stretches

Spinal extension

The spine is central to your awareness and use of the body as a whole.

While it has opportunities to lengthen, following each change of direction in the rowing stroke, it never achieves maximum extension.

The following spinal extension stretch resembles the "cobra" posture in yoga, but *how* to think about carrying it out is crucial, to avoid stress to the neck and lower back:

- Lie prone (face down), with your body lengthened out on the floor, arms resting comfortably on the floor, hands quite close to the head, palms down.

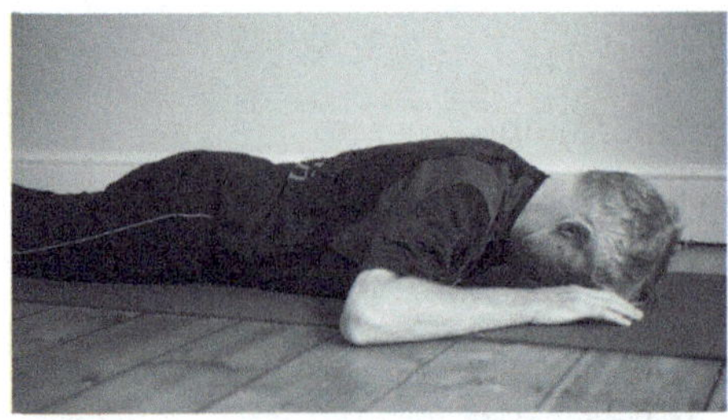

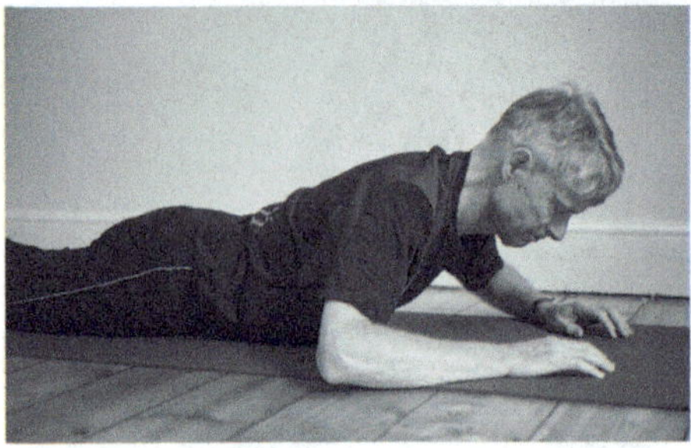

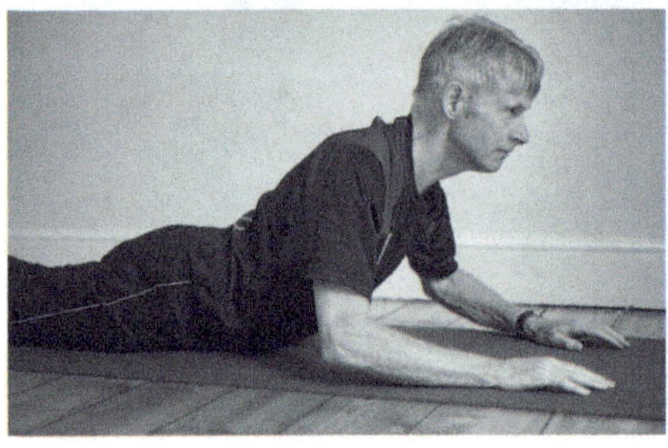

- Invite the neck to release tension and the back to lengthen and widen.
- Raise your upper body by thinking of *lengthening through the front of the chest,* extending the vertebrae in the thoracic (chest region) spine, one by one.
- Then, extend your sense of *lengthening through to the front of the neck,* to let neck and head rise, followed last of all by the eyes. Do not tighten the back of the neck.
- Release back down onto the floor, *lengthening through the back of the spine.*
- Repeat a few times, perhaps rising a little further each time.

▶ Starting from the prone position again, press the thumb-side of the heels of the hands onto the floor to begin raising the body as before.

  - As the arms take some of your body weight, extend not only the upper spine but also, vertebra by vertebra, the lumbar (lower back) spine.
  - As before, let the head follow, eyes last of all, to inhibit any tightening of the neck.
  - Repeat a few times, gradually extending the range of movement.

Shoulders

This is a helpful stretch because the shoulder never gets anywhere near this position in rowing. It also opens the rib cage.

▶ While standing, raise one elbow so that it points upwards, close to the ear, with the hand dropping down onto the shoulder blade.

- Hold this elbow with the other hand and draw it *upwards* as the hand slides *down* the back.
- Keep the neck free of tension and engage your core.
- Feel the ribs separating away from each other but avoid flaring the ribs or arching the lower back.
- Repeat on the other side.

Forearms and fingers

- Stand a little away from a door or wall and bring your palms in contact with it, at just a little below shoulder level to start with.
  - Turn your hands out so that your fingers are pointing *down* and the heels of the hands are *up*.
  - Press your hands against the wall, but keep your shoulders relaxed. Move the hands a little higher for a stronger stretch.
- Alternatively, kneel on all-fours, with the hands turned out as before, your palms resting on the floor under your shoulders and the fingers pointing back to your knees.
  - Rock gently further back to increase the stretch.

Quads

These are the large muscles on the front of the upper thighs. Along with the glutes, they generate the most power in rowing.

- The easiest way to stretch the quads is to lie on your side, with your head supported by the lower hand.
  - With your other hand, take hold of the lower leg close to the ankle and, directing the knee away from the head, draw the leg back.

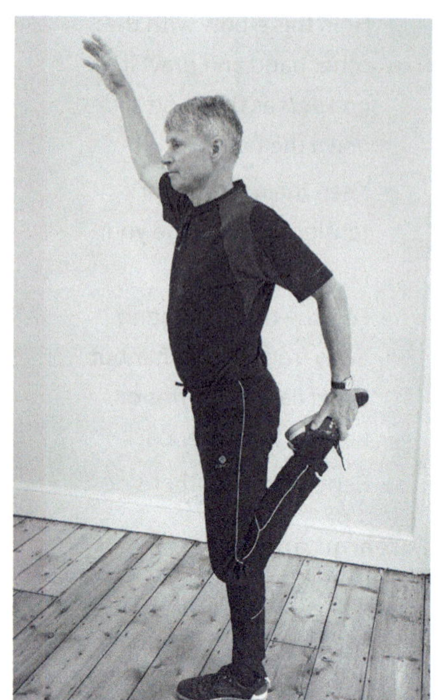

- A more demanding way – but good for the core muscles and for balance – is to stand on one leg, with the fingers of one hand resting lightly against a wall or pointing upwards for balance.
    - Again, with your other hand, take hold of the lower leg close to the ankle.
    - Stand tall and – engaging your core – direct the knee *downwards* while drawing the leg *back*.

Glutes

These are the large buttock muscles that extend the hips and contribute greatly to the power of the drive, as the thrust from the quads diminishes.

- Lie in the AT releasing position with your legs bent and feet flat (as described in Chapter 5).
    - Draw the right knee up and cross the outside of the ankle to the outside of the left thigh, "nestling" it close to the knee.
    - Lengthen your right arm outwards from the shoulder so that it rests along the floor to that side, for stability, palm facing up.
    - With your left hand on the outside of the shin bone, draw the right knee towards the left side of the chest.
    - Apply gentle pressure and feel the stretch in the right glutes.
- Repeat on the other side.

In the next chapter, rowing as a sport – and some of the issues that arise – will be discussed from the point of view of the Alexander Technique (AT).

PART 4

10

Alexander Technique and the sport of rowing

Rowing is a sport marked by nuance;
that's where it departs from exercise.

Frank Cunningham

At the highest levels, the sport of rowing places huge demands on the athlete. National teams nowadays have a panoply of support staff including sports scientists, medics, physios, strength and conditioning coaches, and so on. Rowers are offered Pilates classes and Yoga, with the aim of improving core strength and flexibility. But is that enough?

Injuries in rowers

The main injuries affecting rowers are to the lower back, ribs, and wrists/forearms. Over a twelve-month period, two out of every three adult rowers suffer from lower back pain, compared with one out of three non-rowers. The causes, according to the review paper summarised by World Rowing[1], are:

- High volumes of training – especially on the ergometer.
- Transition times between ergometer and the boat.
- Lack of anterior rotation of the pelvis at catch, plus extreme C-shaped spines which can load the lumbar spine more than four times the rower's mass.

Their recommendation is to be cautious about rowing for longer than half an hour on the ergo. The reviewers do not rate static core stability exercises like the plank but call for more dynamic endurance-based work to prevent injury. They state there is no "proven" way to prevent back injury.

Elite rowers can be tempted to conceal that they are hurting because they might be deselected. *The question as to why rowing, with proper technique, should not strengthen the back, doesn't appear to be raised.* Both Cunningham and Fairbairn emphasised the duty of care to the athlete; and they encouraged their rowers to take responsibility for their own body use.

So, on the one hand, we have the sport of rowing, where winning at almost all costs seems to be the most important thing. On the other hand, Alexander's Technique is all about commitment to the process of finessing coordination of mind and body. Ends versus means. These could be seen as oil and water...but water usually finds a way.

I have tried to show that applying the Alexander Technique can make a major contribution to preventing injury, as well as enhancing the enjoyment of rowing and improving performance in the sport.

How much has changed in the sport of rowing since this photo was taken of the Oxford Boat Crew in training for the Oxford-Cambridge Boat Race, early in 1939? It was included in FM Alexander's last book, *The Universal Constant in Living* (1941), the title of which refers to the way that coordination is often disturbed in many people, in carrying out everyday activities[2].

The caption accompanying the photo, originally published in the *Evening Standard*, read: "Determination mirrored on their faces."

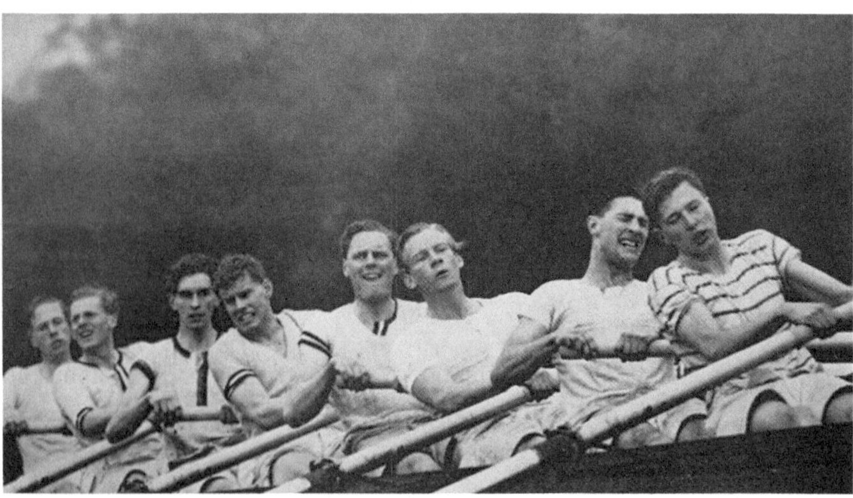

This was Alexander's interpretation:

> Four of them look as if they were being tortured on the rack, three, as if in a trance and just one, the third from the left, as if he had taken part in a rowing race and had the right attitude towards a rowing contest.
>
> Surely a university boat race should be a friendly contest between men animated by the sporting instinct. Every one of them should wish the victory to go to the best crew. It should be an experience of pleasure, happiness and healthy recreation to all concerned, not an unnatural struggle involving distortion and loss of consciousness through the "determination" to gain an end even at the cost of personal exhaustion and damage.
>
> What difference does it really make in the long run whether an Oxford or Cambridge crew wins the boat race in a particular year? In the interest of all concerned, it were far better if we engaged in sport for sport's sake. End-gaining in sport, as in every sphere of life, is in the long view a delusion and snare[2].

In the lead up to the Athens Olympics of 2004, the Amateur Rowing Association of Great Britain – as it was then – commissioned a pilot scheme for nine members of the GB squad to have lessons in the Alexander Technique.

AT teacher Patrick Pearson (also a rowing coach) was involved at the beginning, and his colleague Caroline Chisholm saw the project through.

She wrote:

> I was faced with oarsmen who had an almost religious belief in the contracted muscle, an over-trained physique and an immune system on the blink...they are not good at sensing change or release in their muscles.
>
> Rowers are taught to pull their heads back while lifting weights. When asked to inhibit this, there are surprised smiles as they begin to experience the ease with which they can now lift. ▸

In the main, rowers' use afloat is painful to observe. It is heart-breaking to see the legacy of damage that they are accumulating for later life. This is my number one motivation for continuing with this work, even when the odds seem to be stacked against change.

On the river here in Henley, I see many chronically collapsed spines. To encourage a rower to pivot forward using the hip joint, rather than using the waist as though it is a joint, is a slow, gradual process. [It] gives them several inches more length in the spine. This enables them to make longer and more powerful strokes, thus moving the boat further and faster to win gold[3].

From left: Matthew Pinsent, Ed Coode, James Cracknell and Steve Williams
Photo Courtesy PA Photos

Can you guess which oarsmen had received Alexander lessons?

The lengths to which rowers are prepared to go, in pursuit of winning, was demonstrated at the Boat Race in 2012. The bow man in the Oxford boat collapsed and was hospitalised. He had completely lost consciousness as he pushed himself beyond his limits, when one of Oxford's oars broke in a clash with Cambridge, and their boat was disabled.

An unpublished letter

In the same year, I submitted a version of the following letter to the editor of British Rowing magazine, *Rowing & Regatta,* just before the 2012 London Olympics. They were initially very keen to publish and forwarded it to the coaching team at British Rowing for a response. Apparently, they did respond… but the response was never received:

I was looking back over the April issue (2012) of *Rowing & Regatta* when I was struck by a photograph in the coaching section, of two top women rowers, captioned: "...demonstrate perfect posture at the finish".

This is somewhat ironic because one of them had just been interviewed on the BBC, unable to compete in the first World Cup this year because of a back injury. "It is one of those things that happens to rowers", she said, ***"but we [that is, British Rowing] are quite good at dealing with it"*** (my added emphasis).

Coincidentally, in the same issue the letter of the month raised serious questions about poor back posture at all levels of rowing, and queried whether sufficient attention is given to the injury-prevention function of the proper use of the back.

Perhaps we need to think beyond "posture" and correct positions and seek to understand how the back functions dynamically in the rowing stroke? How can the spine elongate itself both in the drive and the recovery phases of the stroke, gathering itself at front and back stops? The poise of the head on the neck may be crucial in allowing this dynamic to take place freely. Unfortunately, disturbance to the relationship between head, neck and back is common and most of us have very little awareness of it.

In one of the rowers, the head appears to pull down and her neck forwards, at the finish of the stroke. This compresses the lumbar spine, especially if the body swing is close to a 45° layback, directly over the coccyx. Back in action in a later race, this tendency was still apparent in slow-action replay. In addition, shortly after the beginning of the drive phase, the head was frequently jerked back, tightening the neck in the opposite direction and impacting lower down the spine.

My observations may seem irrelevant; at the end of the day the main focus is going to be on how effectively the blades are applied and released, and how fast the boat moves. However, at the very least, harmful patterns of movement will not contribute to going faster and if the rower is stressing the spine unduly, however good rehabilitation might be, they may continue to be risking further incapacity.

A postscript: closer to the Olympics, the rower's tendency to jam her neck was much less obvious; perhaps she had been alerted to the issue by her coaches? The pair went on to win gold in the women's double sculls.

Working with elite rowers

from an interview with AT teacher and movement coach Stefanie Buller

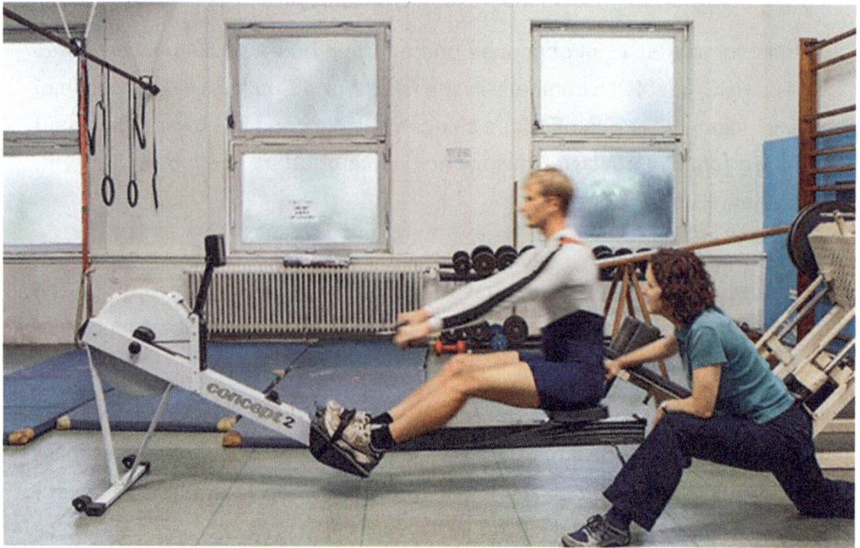

Photo courtesy of Claudia Aguilar-Cruz

This book is all about rowing well on an indoor rower – for fitness, enjoyment, preparing to row on water – and even finding a meditative experience within the beautiful cyclical motion.

Both the Alexander Technique and Tai-chi are movement disciplines with a quiet, attentive quality. The Tai-chi form is slow-moving, allowing time to register when tension is created and, from this awareness, to be able to release it. The Alexander Technique teaches the practice of noticing habitual stressful patterns in any movement, and entertaining the possibility of replacing them with new, easier ones.

But what about competitive rowing? When there is a need "to be tough, and bring everything on the line" in an Olympic race, how is "ease" relevant?

A chance encounter

I spoke with Stefanie Buller, a German psychologist, AT teacher, and movement coach. In recent years she has worked intensively with some competitive rowers in Germany, Switzerland, and Austria, and contributed to their development and successes.

And it all came about by chance: she was helping a young student with his coordination issues when his mother, who was a rowing coach, spotted the potential of applying AT ideas to rowing.

Having worked mainly with musicians, as AT teachers often do, Stefanie knew nothing about rowing technique at this stage, and had no conception – if such a thing exists – of an *ideal* rowing action. What followed was a pilot project with a university student who was a rower. The results were recorded and published in the German Rowing Association magazine in 2014.

Working with Olympians

Following this, she helped to prepare Swiss Nico Stahlberg for his place in a quad in the Rio Olympics (2016), and his success as the overall World Cup winner in the single sculls in 2017. Because of the distance involved, she conducted her coaching by video link, which – in the pre-pandemic era – was considered impossible.

The improvements Stahlberg experienced led to Stefanie being invited, by the head coach of the Swiss men's quad, to lead an intensive weekend workshop with the men's four, in preparation for the Olympics in Rio.

She gave an interactive presentation at the 2016 German National Rowing Association's Conference for Coaches, where Robert Sens – the German State coach of Rhineland-Palatinate – became interested in Stefanie's approach. This led to her contribution to the training of Jason Osborne, who became the World Champion in the lightweight single sculls in 2018.

But surely talking about ease, relaxation, and reduced effort is in apparent contradiction to the toughness required in competition?

Lessons for mind and body

According to Stefanie, the key to working with elite rowers is to address their striving for efficiency – to achieve maximum boat speed with the minimum amount of effort.

Strength and endurance training is often led by a "more-is-more" philosophy. Measuring catch, extraction and the way the blade enters the water, is precisely monitored, to improve the stroke. And while the importance of hip position or angle is also considered, there is less precision in being able to identify where the hip joint – the crucial pivot joint – is located in the body.

Once she has clarified this "mis-mapping," Stefanie begins a process of exploration of the rowing action – so familiar to athletes and coaches – which can now be re-discovered from a new perspective.

Knowing their own hip joints "from the inside-out" is essential, for rowers to achieve the transition from a slight posterior pelvic tilt – at the end of the drive – to a forward tilt in the recovery. This is the most significant aspect of the main body movement that the rower should make in the rowing stroke.

One rower framed it like this:

> *"The decisive realisation was that many joints are somewhere else in my body than I thought they were. I was then able to better control the levers that work when rowing...As soon as my inner concepts matched the anatomical reality, the forces acted more directly."*

In individual and group sessions, Stefanie guides athletes and coaches through a process of re-discovery, an experience of changed movement quality which, in turn, will often lead to new questions.

In later stages, when trust has been established, she finds that deeper questions can be addressed: difficult emotions, conflicts in the team, fears of failure or traces of traumatic events – for instance, with bullying coaches or physical injury that can still affect movement quality in the present moment.

Balancing ease and power application

The recovery phase of the rowing stroke is an issue that becomes more important at the top levels of competition. Margins are narrow, and work on applying power effectively can only go so far. Letting the boat "fly" during the recovery – preparing for the next stroke without unintentionally slowing the boat – then becomes extremely important.

AT and Tai-chi offer great benefits in achieving these aims: an ability to be calm and attentive, and an invitation to sense what´s going on in body and mind. In the end, it´s about understanding a paradox: while working harder, pushing harder, and becoming stronger, a parallel process needs to take place – an exploration of how the same power output can be achieved with less effort and less tension. Stefanie finds that this concept – which she calls "constructive laziness"– is highly provocative for many young, ambitious athletes. That is, until they become hooked on their first positive experiences with it.

Tuning in to subtle bodily sensations is not the forte of many athletes. Countless hours of strength training or on-the-bike conditioning can cause athletes to mistake tension for strength. But muscles are strong when they can move through their full range of length. A tense muscle is a weak muscle. Therefore, an athlete, despite being extremely strong, can be limited in their performance because of an inability to let go of excessive muscle tension.

One way Stefanie works with an athlete is to help them identify a tense area in the body, then consciously tense it even more – and then stop tensing – to allow the necessary release.

Releasing tension and pain

Stefanie shared an anecdote: an exceptionally strong athlete experienced his Eureka moment when he could feel how his connection to the water – simulated by her working with her hands – became stronger and more intense with a release in his arms.

For the first time, he found he could feel a connection all the way through his body, and how directional forces in the body work in opposition to each other. He knew that many coaches had told him to be "looser" or "less tense," but now he had a real experience of what it felt like. Being complimented on the reduction in his overall muscle tension by the physiotherapist was then just an additional bonus.

Stefanie observes that elite rowers also have a "weird" relationship with pain. "No pain, no gain" is a common mantra to push through hard sessions and the pain resulting from the build-up of lactic acid in muscles is seen as an indicator that they're "in the zone." Enduring this pain better than their competitors can even help them succeed.

Musculo-skeletal pain is a different issue, though, as the athlete may either neglect it, or try to "muscle through it," and risk injury. Or they may over-react to their pain. Teaching body sensitivity to rowers can be a double-edged sword. They must learn to distinguish between using it to develop their stroke and then being able to push through – and not "bottling out in the tunnel of pain" that can occur in a race.

Stefanie gave an example of how a rower tweaked a muscle by making an awkward movement after an exhausting training session. "This can lead to a kind of panic-mode for athletes and coaches," she says, as it could lead to a rower missing training.

She explained to the rower how over-dramatising can increase pain and tension, and how calming the nervous system can be as simple as going for a walk – though this was "a very unattractive activity for an Olympic rower." However, he reluctantly agreed to follow her advice. On returning, it was clear from the way he was walking that he was no longer in pain. He gave her the thumbs-up and resumed his place in the boat the next day.

The hidden force of habit

Coaches like Robert Sens – who was appointed national head coach of Austrian Rowing in 2020 – can see the potential that this process of re-evaluation offers a team.

Austria is renowned for its skiing, but not so much for its rowing. Sens has taken on the challenge of developing Austrian Rowing to the next level, starting with the youngest rowers. Agreeing on the main technical elements of the rowing stroke is vital for crew-rowing because, to make the boat "sing," all the rowers in a boat must harmonise their rowing action. This includes finding consensus on the key features of the human body and how it moves best.

Good coaches understand their responsibility towards young people. They also know that, of the many who commit to training, only a few will make it to the top. However, this duty of care includes the well-being of *all* athletes, not just a few. Years later, many masters rowers come to realise the toll the sport has taken on their bodies.

In the end, an athlete is human, although they may achieve what appears to be superhuman. Such a performance is more than the sum of its parts. Even taking into account genetic advantage, the hours of training and all that is involved, there´s something else that connects all of that together, which is the history and experience of an individual. "It's as if, when it all comes together in performance, 1 + 1 = 3."

Just like a good team is more than the sum of its parts, the same is true for a human organism. This "connective tissue" of behaviour is invisible and defies scientific measurement. It is therefore often overlooked in high performers, although very experienced coaches may have a sense of this from their own experience.

What the Alexander Technique uniquely offers is a systematic approach to this invisible connective tissue called "habit." Alexander teachers have developed – and employ – finely-honed powers of observation and skilled hands-on work. With these, they can assist an athlete to experience *directly* what is required.

Stefanie is also currently completing a Master's degree in psychology. Expanding her neurological and psychological knowledge helps her develop an even more holistic understanding of how mind and body interact. She helps an individual – whatever their particular sport or occupation is – identify the often-unconscious thinking and emotions that underlie their patterns of movement.

Learning and development never stop. Dedication to a sport, or any activity, requires a continuous reshaping of habits. When the world-famous cellist Pablo Casals was asked, at age 80, why he continued to practice for up to five hours a day, he answered, "Because I think I am making progress."

Practice makes it permanent. When Michael Phelps was filmed warming up in a practice pool, prior to a butterfly stroke final at the 2012 London Olympics, he was barely making a splash. To use a cliché, he was "poetry in motion." It is possible to discover this sense of ease in almost any discipline.

The main theme of this book is finding "form" in rowing – what it is, how to create and maintain it, and how to recover it when you lose it.

Striving to win at all costs, without the necessary groundwork, goes against form.

If you are unable to row slowly, efficiently, with ease, and with some elegance, you will never sustain your form at speed and under pressure.

British rower Steve Redgrave, a five-time Olympic gold medallist, said that the secret to his success was "relaxation". What is **true** relaxation? **That** is our exploration.

Coastal rowing is one of the new areas of growth in rowing. Another is *indoor rowing competition*, which has really taken off in recent years: however, it's hard to see any grace in this new sport. At the end of the day, though, it depends what "floats your boat."

This book has tried to promote the value of *re-creational* rowing, indoors as well as on-the-water.

The focus of the final chapter, then, is about venturing onto waterways for pleasure; and outlines the benefits of complementary forms of whole mind-body exercise, including walking and running, swimming and Tai-chi.

11

Beyond indoor rowing

Any activity that you attempt challenges your ability to coordinate yourself, whether it's Argentine tango, or skiing, or any of the mind-body forms of exercise explored later in this chapter. One of the many benefits of embracing a new pursuit can be a growing confidence in your ability to coordinate yourself generally, whatever your age.

On becoming a sculler

Extraordinary as it seems to me now, my experience of the indoor rower for nearly two years was so satisfying that I had not given any thought to venturing out on water.

I had come across a wonderful book – a meditation on rowing – by American historian Barry Strauss, *Rowing against the Current: on learning to scull at 40*[1]. At the time I was already well into my fifties, short and slight, and had only been out in a single scull once, in my early twenties. Looking back, I'm surprised that I didn't capsize! My prevailing image of the sport had been that of the Boat Race, the gladiatorial contest between the young, athletic crews of Oxford and Cambridge Universities. I had no interest, unlike Professor Strauss, in competitive racing.

One day, on a run around a small Norfolk broad near home, I noticed scullers out on the river Yare, which meanders nearby. They looked as though they were enjoying themselves, and it occurred to me: *why wasn't I out there, too, having fun?* I made enquiries, and joined Yare Boat Club in Norwich, where recreational rowers were welcomed.

I believed – foolishly as it turned out – that I would make the transition from indoor rowing to sculling without a hitch. I only had to add the whole business

of getting the oars in and out of the water – which I'd not considered at all, up to that point – to the general body movement I'd been cultivating on the indoor rower.

Many folks are drawn to the Alexander Technique (AT) because they recognise that they are not so well coordinated and need to address that issue. And it was suggested that, with my knowledge of the AT – and also Tai-chi – I would find the business of balancing the boat, a single scull, relatively easy. I had, however, grossly underestimated my tendency to *un*balance the boat, due largely to a case of sloppy blade-work.

The sun shone, there was a light breeze – unusual weather for March – and I loved being out on the water. I made some progress in the early months and then enrolled on a five-day course, with a view to making further improvement. On my return, it was quite clear I had not progressed and was, if anything, somewhat worse.

However much I tried, I could not seem to get the blades cleanly out of the water, despite being constantly urged to "tap down" more quickly at the release. And on the recovery, I was told I was not squaring my blades early enough, in preparation for the drive.

These instructions are part of mainstream thinking on rowing technique, especially in Britain. I became so discouraged by my failure to develop the ease I wanted, that I nearly gave up at that stage.

In my hour of need, I took a second look at one of the books recommended by Barry Strauss. The book was *The Sculler at Ease*, by Frank Cunningham. I'd discounted it at first because it was so much at odds with standard rowing fare. It begins with the clearest account of what is necessary to develop the skill of oarsmanship: how the hands – and particularly the fingers – control the handles, and therefore the blades.

I was intrigued by the zen-like description of the release of the blades from the water. The "puddles" – the evidence, in the water, of the blades leaving – will show...

> *...very little broken white water around [them]. You will come to know the sound of a clean release.*

Three sculling drills

Cunningham sets out drills to help you towards mastery. Here are a few you might like to try if you can get out on water.

1. One-arm sculling

Practicing this drill can greatly improve balance and symmetry in sculling:

- In the boat, with your legs down, lay one blade *feathered* on the water, for balance, and focus on the blade work of the other one.

This drill, one of Cunningham's favourites, immediately revealed how untidy my blade work was, especially on the right. Perhaps it was not surprising that my right arm caused most of the problems: I was very right-side dominant and used to a lot of "doing". My left arm, not "knowing" what to do, just seemed to find its way more easily.

This drill is a very effective way to focus on the *quality* of entry, and release of the blade, on each side. Naturally, you will go round in circles – which is not much of an issue on a lake or wide stretch of water. But on a narrower river, you may only have space to do two or three strokes to one side, before doing the same on the other side. And you will need to keep a sharp lookout for other boats on the river.

2. The four-inch drive

This is a great way to throw caution to the winds and find spontaneity at the catch. The "four-inch" refers to cutting off the stroke – abruptly shortening it – at the very beginning of the drive. You can risk it going wrong:

- Start by sitting poised at full slide, with your blades feathered on the water and with the lightest hold on the handles.
  - To start the drive, without lunging forwards, press the *inside of the heels down* and instantly turn the handles by rolling the fingers, to slice the blades into the water.
  - Your fingers respond more quickly than the bigger muscle groups, and the consequence is to exactly synchronise the catch with the beginning of the drive.
  - The idea in this drill is to start the drive – and then to immediately abort mission.
  - If your hold is like "gossamer", as Cunningham describes it, the handles will continue to roll under your fingers as the blades square quickly under water pressure.
  - If one or both blades slice in too deeply, or do not connect properly to the water, your relatively "non-doing" fingers can register that fact; and anyway, as pressure is released quickly, the boat will not tip.
  - Repeat this with the boat stationary, and then while the shell is in motion, with your blades feathered off the water, balancing the boat.

3. The 12-ounce drive

This is a great way to sense total body connection at catch, and to experience how the blades – if permitted – will travel through the water at the right depth.

- Start as in the previous drill, but – as soon as the blades enter the water – do *not* apply any pressure.
  - Let the blades find their way through the water, as if in slow motion.
  - Release the blades easily from the water, at the end of the drive, by using the shoulders to draw the handles in, and rolling the fingers away.

As my sculling progressed, and the years passed, my Raynaud's disease (often called "dead man's fingers") worsened, and I was no longer able to safely row in the winter.

However, I continued indoor rowing during the cold months, as many rowers do. I used the time to visualise how the rolling in and out of my fingers would produce the oarsmanship that I wanted in the boat.

When I first went out again on the river in spring, I thought it would be a mixed experience, to say the least. To my delight, however, it was as though there had never been those long winter months of lay-off.

Beyond Rowing

Although rowing is a wonderful whole-body exercise, using a very important range of movement, it doesn't do everything. There is no spinal rotation – except in sweep oar, though that's one-sided – or rotation at other joints. Nor does it afford a complete range of movement at all the joints.

Especially as you age, it's good to be familiar with a diverse range of activities to maintain optimal fitness. These can be drawn on as personal preference, need, circumstance and whim dictate.

Cross-training – maintaining fitness by activities other than their main sport – is an important part of the rehabilitation of athletes, while recovering from injury. But how about *preventing* injury in the first place?

Cycling is a great "incidental" exercise, getting you from A to B in a commute, often more quickly than by car in busy urban environments. It's a good way to keep the legs in shape if you have rowing injuries, and it helps maintain cardio-vascular fitness. However, muscular work is restricted to the legs. For that reason, it is quite limited and competitive cyclists suffer a lot of injuries, quite apart from the risk of accidents on the road.

Acquiring skill over a range of activities develops sound fitness. The phrase in Latin, *mens sana in corpore sano* (a healthy mind in a healthy body), points to the holistic nature of fitness and well-being. Taking on new challenges – or re-visiting an old one – can develop brain plasticity, as well as facilitating more harmony and balance in the body.

Steve Fairbairn, the so-called "father of modern rowing", was a multi-talented athlete and sportsman in his younger days. He encouraged his rowers to take healthy exercise, especially walking and running, to supplement their rowing training.

Walking and Running

What could be more fundamental and natural than walking?

In addition to the bending and lifting movement pattern intrinsic to the rowing action – managing the vertical plane when on your feet – walking and running were the fundamental survival activities of hunter-gatherers that involved horizontal movement.

But modern man and woman do not always move well, and few people have much idea of how they might improve their locomotion.

Walking and/or running on a treadmill is acceptable if the weather is not conducive to outdoor activity. However, it is a poor substitute for the challenge of constantly adjusting to changing conditions outside and under the feet, and the need to stay alert to potential hazards. It's best to avoid wearing headphones: they disconnect you from your body and the environment.

The only special equipment you need are shoes which do not block your feet's sensitivity to the ground, and which foster a range of motion close to a barefoot style.

You could begin with walking, then break into a run for a bit, and then walk again. There's no need to keep running continuously, and a heart monitor can be a great aid in moderating your efforts.

How to play with walking:

- Place one foot very slightly forward of the other.
  - Gaze into the distance to help the head to balance on top of the spine – vital for balance in general.
  - To avoid trip hazards and dog mess, let your eyes glance down from time to time, without pulling the head and neck forwards and downwards.
- Starting with your weight towards the heels, play with leaning forwards the smallest amount from the ankles. And then ease back.
  - Next, as soon as you begin to incline forwards, *press your front foot back,* and the other knee will lift and bring *that* foot underneath you, to save you from falling. And then keep going.
- Notice how, in walking, the outside of the heel can touch *lightly* first (pronation), then roll forward, through to the rest of the foot.
  - Focus on *pressing the inside of your heels backwards* – the force carries through to the big toes (supination) – to sustain the momentum of walking *forwards*.
  - To walk faster, rather than overstriding, *press the heels back for longer*.

The spine needs spiralling movements to stay flexible and healthy:

- If you start with the *left foot slightly in advance of the right foot*, the hips will have automatically rotated to the right.
  - Counter-rotation then needs to take place in the upper body, so *draw the left arm back*.
- To take one small step, *as soon you start to lean, press the left heel back.*
  - And as the *right arm now swings back*, allow the right knee to lift, and you will take one small step, your hips then turning to the *left*.
- Unwind, and then wind up to the *left*, your *left arm drawing back*, and take a small step with the left foot.
- Repeat these small, rather mechanical steps, stopping each time – and then go for it. Don't micro-manage the movement: see if you can now walk more smoothly in continuous motion.

Celebrate the beauty and economy of walking. No wonder early humans became the supreme predator on the planet: bipedalism is energy efficient.

Walking – and running when needed – kept an animal in view or enabled tracks to be followed before they became obscured. When the prey had to keep moving, it would eventually succumb to heat exhaustion.

Running, in comparison with walking, increases energy demands because of leaving the ground: at a point in the running cycle, both feet lose contact and are off the ground.

How then, to run more efficiently? Here are some pointers form AT teacher and running coach Malcolm Balk's *The Art of Running*[2]:

- Standing with feet close together, let the weight shift from just in front of the heels to just behind the balls of the feet, with the heels still in light contact with the ground.
    - Bending the legs a little, load the arches and bounce off the feet. Minimise up and down movement, be light and quick. Compare how easy it is to land on the mid-foot with landing on the heels.
- Next, run on the spot. Bend the elbows, shortening the arm levers to activate the rhythm of the legs.
    - Draw the elbows back – the fingers lightly curled into the palms – and move the hands from "nips to hips".
- As the arms move quickly, lean a little from the ankles and break into a run.

If the landing foot stays too long on the ground, the elastic spring that assists forward motion is lost. So, as in rowing, rhythm and cadence are important. In general, however slowly you are running, aim to take a minimum of 170-180 steps/minute to reduce contact time with the ground. Put a metronome app on your phone to get into the rhythm.

Landing on the mid-foot – the heel touching immediately afterwards – helps spring you forward. It may *feel* as though the feet are landing behind you, especially if are you are used to the braking effect of "heel-striking" with your feet way out in front. Tuning in to the changing pressures on the feet – as suggested in rowing – can make your running action more effective and pleasurable.

Skating

In-line (rollerblading) or ice-skating could help your outdoor rowing by improving your ability to balance on each side in turn – one side of the body often being dominant. Skating, by slowly shifting all the weight onto one leg at a time, can expose and help redress any imbalance.

Most important of all, experience the kinetic chain of energy generated from the ground up:

- Push off one leg – transferring weight to the other – loading the arch on that side:
    - This sets in motion a wonderful feeling, a "zing" of energy flowing up from the ground to the leg and into the pelvis, which is free to swing sideways as well as forwards and backwards a little – a much fuller range of motion than rowing – then up the spine and out to the arms.

Swimming

Immersion in water can facilitate the letting go which may be harder to achieve in the field of gravity. When Barry Strauss was injured from the excesses of competitive zeal, his rehabilitation entailed transforming his rowing action on the indoor rower – and swimming: this helped relieve the pressure on his damaged intervertebral discs and allowed his spine to fully elongate in its weightless state.

Of course, to be able to row safely outdoors requires the ability to swim some distance in the event of a capsize. Even apparently competent swimmers may carry a residual fear of water, often for good reasons – not least of which is the threat of hypothermia.

However, allowing yourself to be immersed in water at a comfortable temperature can help dissolve tension patterns. Bear in mind that the human body is over two-thirds water, and that water can have an immensely calming effect. Humans, along with aquatic mammals such as seals and dolphins, have a "diving reflex". Immersion starts to lower heart rate and blood pressure.

Try this in a shallow pool, and wear goggles that provide a leak-proof, clear and wide field of vision, so that you can more easily orientate yourself:

Floating

- Find out how buoyant you are generally – and which parts float easily.
    - Easing into the water, allow your head to be completely supported by it, lifting your feet off the bottom...not going anywhere to start with... looking directly down.
    - Breathe out quietly, blowing the gentlest bubbles.
    - Then *fold* your body, to get your feet underneath you again, to stand up.

Gliding

- Present a long sleek profile to glide through the water with the least resistance. Ease into the water as follows and see how little you can disturb it:
  - Take a step forward, leaning forwards and saying "yes" to the water, easing in, looking down, letting your arms sweep through under water, directing them forwards and slightly downward.
  - Let your fingers be loose, lower than your relaxed wrists, which are lower than your elbows, and lower than the shoulders.
  - Lift your legs towards the surface, bringing them together.
  - Again, breathe out the gentlest of bubbles. Look directly down to the bottom of the pool, with your neck and spine long and your back broad.
  - How far can you glide before your legs start to sink?
- To return to standing:
  - Instead of lifting your head first, look back along your body to your feet.
  - Then, bending the knees, press the arms downward and backwards to draw your hips and feet forward. Watch your feet landing underneath you.
  - Press your feet into the floor and stand, relaxing the shoulders at the end to let the head rebalance itself.
  - Let the breath in.

Front crawl and backstroke, swum well, are based on spiralling movements; breaststroke and butterfly cultivate flexion and extension of the spine. The spine needs all of its range of movement possibilities.

The Art of Swimming[3] – based on AT principles – and *Total Immersion*[4], are radically different approaches to swimming that pay close attention to the process of learning and promote use of the limbs *in the context of the core of the body*.

A "sculling" backstroke

To sustain momentum and swim, you must **hold on to** the water, to move your body forward.

This is the same idea as in the boat, locking blades into the water and prising the boat past the blades. Is the aim to move the river backwards, or the boat forwards?

To hold the water, allow the joints of your arms to bend. Forearms, hands, and fingers – slightly apart – act as paddles, and lever your body forward.

Inevitably there will be some slippage, but it makes all the difference to ask if your intention is to move water, or to move yourself?

In the meantime, on your back in the water, play with my novel sculling version of the "old English" or "elementary" backstroke.

Think of your arms long, like oars, which can be squared under water, and, in the recovery, the palms, turned up – or "feathered" – can skim over the surface of the water:

- Bend your legs a little to "sit" in the water.
  - Then lean slowly backwards, lifting the feet up to the surface – as if you were on a reclining chair – and rest your head on the water. Bring the legs together.
  - At the same time sweep the arms over the water, with palms up, allowing them to move gently out to the side and behind you.
- While still gliding, drop the feet a little from the knees, turning them out…
  - Then press the feet away and squeeze the legs together, drawing the feet close to each other.

- At the same time, slice the little fingers into the water and press the hands back – which will square if the wrists are relaxed – in a soft propulsive action just under the surface of the water. Don't drive them back very far.

- To recover the arms, let the thumbs lead the rotation of the forearm, and the little fingers slice out.
  - The arms will recover over the surface, "feathered"; the legs stay together as you glide.

This is a wonderfully relaxing way to move through the water.

Tai-chi

If coordination skills were to be graded in order of difficulty, it's likely that walking/running would be easiest to improve.

Indoor rowing is a little harder, followed by single sculling making significantly more demands. Learning to swim the four main strokes sustainably requires a fuller range of skills.

A much higher level of skill is required in Tai-chi or any of the "internal" martial arts, where the underlying ideas – as opposed to applying physical force – are fundamental. Some of the concepts applied to rowing in this book derive directly from Yeung family Tai-chi. This relatively new teaching – outside of the family – is gradually being transmitted in the West[5].

My four pillars of physical exercise are:

- walking/running
- rowing – both indoor and on water
- swimming
- Tai-chi

Coordination skills can be improved over the years, like good wine, even as age and decrepitude threaten. With patient application, you can delay creeping stiffness, dwindling muscle mass and declining endurance.

My hope is that this book, as well as inspiring you to want to row well, encourages you to be open to a wide range of activities which can help you to move more, function better and experience more healthy years in a longer life.

Notes & Resources

Notes

Chapter 1 On rowing and some influential rowers

1 **Mallory**, Peter, *The Sport of Rowing*, River and Rowing Museum, 2011.

2 **Joy**, Jimmy, *Hanlan's Spirit: training for flow,* Lulu Press, Inc., 2011.

3 **Fairbairn**, Steve, *On Rowing*.

4 **Cuningham**, Frank, *The Sculler at Ease,* Avebury Press, *1992*.

5 Thames Watermen sculling style (flip catch) by Sherri **Cassuto**.
Filmed just before she died, the former Olympian, with her take on what Frank Cunningham taught her:
https://www.youtube.com/watch?v=vXHYPUY2QqI

Chapter 2 The Rowing Stroke: primer

1 M1x FINAL A, **Manson**, Robert, WRC II Poznan 2017, WBT- 6:30.74:
https://www.youtube.com/watch?v=plXhvUJoVMY&t=281s

Chapter 4 User's manual

1 **Dobie**, Gwen, *Rowing for Gold*, STATnews, Vol 5, no 6, Jan 2000.

2 **Alexander**, FM, *The Use of the Self*, Orion Spring, 2018 (first edition 1932).

Chapter 7 The whole stroke … and nothing but

1 **Cassuto**, Sherri, Thames Watermen sculling style (flip catch) Sherri Cassuto, US National Team. Single Sculler 198w
https://www.youtube.com/watch?v=vXHYPUY2QqI

3 BladeBoatBody, Goofs RC, YouTube, Frank Cunningham in action, with expert commentary by Stan **Pocock**
be.com/watch?v=6KJkFZI8v5w&t=11shttps://

4 The Sculler's Hand & Blade, 3riversrowing, YouTube, original video made in 1975 by Frank **Cunningham** and Stan **Pocock**

Chapter 10 Alexander technique and the sport of rowing

1 *2021 consensus statement for preventing and managing low back pain in elite and sub elite adult rowers*, British Journal of Sports Medicine, February 2021.

2 **Alexander**, FM, *The Universal Constant in Living*, first edition 1941.

3 **Chisholm**, Caroline, *Olympic gold for FM Alexander*, STATnews, October 2004.

Chapter 11 Beyond indoor rowing

1 **Strauss**, Barry, *Rowing against the Current: on learning to scull at 40*, Prentice Hall & IBD,1 1999

2 **Balk**, Malcolm, Master the Art of Running, Collins and Brown, 2007. Also visit: **https://www.theartofrunning.com**

3 **Shaw**, Steven, Master the Art of Swimming, Collins and Brown, 2006. Also visit: **https://www.artofswimming.com**

4 Visit: **https://www.totalimersion.net**

Resources

Rowing

Boyne, Daniel, *Essential Sculling*, The Lyons Press; 2nd edition 2020

Brink, van den, H. M., *On the Water*, translated from the Dutch by Vincent, Paul, London: Faber and Faber, 2001 (originally published in Dutch in 1998).
A haunting novella about a summer of happiness as young men from very different backgrounds and their mysterious coach create a winning pair – the hardest crew boat to race – set against the background of impending war. It was to be made into a feature film and, perhaps now that Boys in the Boat has been successful on the screen, this project will be revived.

Brown, Daniel James, *The Boys in the Boat*, MacMillan, 2013.
Brown uncovered the story of Joe Rantz, one of a group of working-class men who rowed successfully the American eight in the 1936 Olympics in Berlin, now made into a major feature film by George Clooney.

Cox, Ian, *Tao in the Art of Rowing: an Alpha to Zen of Crew*, CreateSpace Independent Publishing Platform, 2015
A serious account of the metaphysics of rowing.

Cunningham, Frank, *The Sculler at Ease*, Avebury Press, 1992.
The classic account of the art of sculling.

Cunningham, Frank, *Ask Frank*, Lake Washinton Rowing Club, 2006.
Musings and Q & As from the LWRC monthly newsletter.

Fairbairn, Ian ed. *Steve Fairbairn on Rowing*, London: The Kingswood Press, 1990.
The collection by the son of his father's writings on rowing.

Joy, Jimmy, *Hanlan's Spirit: Training for Flow*, Lulu Press, 2011.

Joy, James C, *The Quantum Sculler*, Jon/Vanamringe, 2nd edition 2016.
Jimmy Joy brought a deep sense of spiritual connection to an in-depth examination of the parts and flow of the whole rowing stroke.

Lambert, Craig, *Mind over Water: lessons on life from the art of rowing*, Houghton Mifflin, 1999.

Mallory, Peter, The Sport of Rowing: Two Centuries of Competition (four volumes), River and Rowing Museum, Henley, 2011.
A monumental achievement – fully illustrated, including stills from old film footage – celebrating the sport of rowing, rowers and coaches and their thinking on styles of rowing over the years. Originally published in a limited edition, it's available to view – but not to download:
https://worldrowing.com/about/history/the-sport-of-rowing/

Nolte, Volker, ed., Rowing Science: the nexus of knowledge and performance, Human Kinetics, 2024.
The latest research, summarised by leading sports scientists, on all aspects of the sport.

Strauss, Barry, *Rowing Against the Current: on Learning to Scull at 40*, Prentice Hall & IBD, 1999.

Alexander Technique

Alexander, Frederick Matthias, *The Use of the Self*, Orion Spring, 2018 (first edition 1932)
The first chapter, Evolution of a Technique, describes the development of the basic ideas and is a testament to the power of the mind to change everything.

De Alcantara, Pedro, *The Alexander Technique: a Skill for Life*, The Crowood Press Ltd, 2nd edition, 2021.

https://www.alexandertechnique.com
A catalogue of resources, books, articles podcasts, on AT

Tai-chi

www.yeungfamilytaichi.com

www.youtube.com/@yeungfamilytaichi
Because Tai-chi was traditionally transmitted via the relationship between teacher and pupil, there is little written material to recommend; the information that has been made available is often rather mixed.

Videos on the Thames Waterman Stroke:

The Scullers Hand and Blade

https://www.youtube.com/watch?v=E4pxeBp1X9Q

Old, unedited film showing Frank Cunningham and Stan Pocock (son of George).

BladeBoatBody

https://www.youtube.com/watch?v=6KJkFZI8v5w&t=203s

Stan Pocock narrating the "Pocock" stroke aka the Thames Waterman Style with Frank Cunningham, Charlie McIntyre and others demonstrating (From the Guy Harper collection).

Thames Watermen sculling style (flip catch) by Sherri Cassuto:

https://www.youtube.com/watch?v=vXHYPUY2QqI

Filmed just before she died, Sherri Cassuto, former Olympian, with her homage to Frank Cunningham and his teaching.

Made in United States
Orlando, FL
13 March 2025

59427059R00098